Communication, Collaboration and Creativity
Researching Adult Learning

Communication, Collaboration and Creativity
Researching Adult Learning

Edited by
Marianne Horsdal

University Press of Southern Denmark 2010

© The authors and University Press of Southern Denmark 2010
Printed by Grafisk Data Center A/S
Cover Design by Donald Jensen

ISBN 978 87 7674 503 5

University Press of Southern Denmark
Campusvej 55
DK-5230 Odense M
Phone: +45 6615 7999
Fax: +45 6615 8126
www.universitypress.dk

Distribution in the United States and Canada:
International Specialized Book Services
5804 NE Hassalo Street
Portland, OR 97213-3644 USA
www.isbs.com

Distribution in the United Kingdom:
Gazelle
White Cross Mills
Hightown
Lancaster
LA1 4 XS
U.K.
www.gazellebooks.co.uk

Contents

Introduction 7
Marianne Horsdal, University of Southern Denmark

Wider Benefits of Learning within the
Liberal Adult Education System in Finland 17
Jyri Manninen, Joeensu University

Lifelong Learning as Continuity and Transformation.
A Qualitative longitudinal study about adults' biographies
of learning and teaching 37
*Christiane Hof, University of Frankfurt/Main & Monika Fischer,
University of Frankfurt/Main*

Desire as Response to Experience:
Reflections on Motivational Aspects of Adult Learning......... 53
Ulla Thøgersen, University of Aalborg

Social Construction of Meaning and its Translation
into Real World Action: The problem of learning transfer
and how to circumvent it 69
Søren Willert, University of Aalborg

Towards a Substantial Notion of Validation 85
Christina Chaib & Bergmo Prulovic, University of Jönköping

Initial Education and Training of Adult Teachers
and Trainers in Denmark................................. 103
*Anne Larson & Marcella Milana, Danish School of Education,
University of Aarhus*

Quality for Adult Educators? 117
Petros Gougoulakis, Stockholm University

Framing of Collaboration and its Impact
on Creativity and Innovative Skills. 145
Birthe Lund & Annie Aarup Jensen, University of Aalborg

Teacher Teams as (De-) Professionalizing?
– Possible consequences of the 2005 Reform
in the Danish Upper Secondary School 161
*Thomas R. S. Albrechtsen & Dion Rüsselbæk Hansen,
University of Southern Denmark*

Lifelong, Life-wide and Life-deep Learning:
Utilizing the lens of HIV/AIDS in Southern Africa 177
Shirley Walters, University of Western Cape

Authors 191

Introduction

The background for this book is the 3rd Nordic Conference on Adult Learning, which took place 22-24 April 2009 in Denmark hosted by University of Southern Denmark, Institute of Philosophy, Education and the Study of Religions. In the call for papers we announced that the 10 best contributions would be published in this series of educational research and development. The selection of papers for this publication has been extremely difficult as the paper presentations in general had a very high quality as several participants noticed in the closing remarks at the conference. However, I chose to stick to the announced number of selected contributions, but a volume of twice this size, worthy of publication, had not been difficult to produce from the presented papers.

The conference was a sequel to the Nordic conference on adult learning 2005 in Turku, Finland and the Nordic conference on adult learning 2007 in Linköping, Sweden. A book edited by Risto Rinne, Anja Heikkinen & Petri Salo, *Adult Education – Liberty, Fraternity, Equality? Nordic views on lifelong learning* was published after the Finnish conference which actually revived a long tradition of regular encounters between Nordic researchers on adult learning (the research network: Forskning i Norden). The conferences are a meeting-place for Nordic researchers, but we also have and welcome participants from other places in the world. The 3rd conference in Denmark *Communication, Collaboration and Creativity* was attended by participants researching all kinds of aspects of adult learning and education in formal, non-formal or informal settings. And we invited prominent scholars on the international scene as key-note speakers to represent the world outside Europe and to challenge the Nordic perspectives.

The range of research presented in this volume includes a variety of contexts: liberal adult education, workplace learning, higher education, professional development and informal learning, and the theoretical perspectives include a wide but interdependent range of perspectives.

Adult learning in the Nordic countries is viewed through the lens of the individual learners, the adult educators, or the discourses of educational policy documents.

Researchers in Nordic countries have developed strong links for good reasons. Organized learning activities for adults have been a prominent feature for a long time, and Nordic research has established a strong position. Yet, we need to strengthen our links, to communicate and collaborate in order to elaborate understandings of the phenomena we research. We need to enhance creativity through communication and collaboration in research on adult learning, also in an international perspective. The conference was, and this book hopefully will be, an important step in this direction.

There are dual motives for the choice of the theme of the 3rd Nordic Conference. First, in the previous volumes in this series of publications on educational research and development, communication and collaboration across disciplines and institutions and across the usual contexts of theory production and professional practice have often been stressed as a fruitful premise for emergence of creativity and new knowledge (e.g. Gleerup, 2002, 2004). Therefore, we wanted to invite this type of thinking and research in order to enhance our understanding of creativity and emergence of new knowledge as a significant aspect of the role and meaning of adult learning. Communication, collaboration and creativity are interdependent aspects, and we need more research to inform us of the complex ways they work together in the process of learning in various contexts.

The second motive originated in a discussion at a valorization conference organized by the European Commission which presented the selected projects on intercultural dialogue. Someone said in one of the closing remarks that it was not enough just to acknowledge diversity, or to engage in a dialogue across cultures, but we had to collaborate, to do things together in order to develop our understanding. 2008 was European year of Intercultural dialogue, and 2009 was European year of Creativity and innovation. Some of the selected projects in 2009 specifically promoted this kind of intercultural collaboration in very creative ways.

Inspired by this, and considering the very broad range of adult learning, the idea has been to organize a conference and to produce a book where the different perspectives on adult learning may broaden our understanding as we try to capture the richly faceted image of adult learning in full.

The title of the first chapter "Wider Benefits of Learning" points at a general assumption manifested in the overall conception of this book. As adult educators and researchers of adult learning we should neither confine ourselves to a narrow conception on adult learning nor to a narrow perspective on the outcomes of learning but be attentive to maintenance of a wide concept of learning and to the wider benefits of learning.

The research represented in Manninen's article, "Wider Benefits of Learning", is central to the field of adult learning in its attempt to define the role and meaning of participation in liberal adult education, which is still – we claim – a significant part of lifelong learning, not least in the Nordic countries.

While the *Memorandum on lifelong learning* (2000) acknowledged four dimensions of outcomes of lifelong learning: personal development, employability, active citizenship, and social inclusion, educational policies during the last decade often tend to decrease the focus to the issue of employability in spite of the fact that the narrow perspective on learning outcomes has been criticized in the same period, (See for example the publication by Schuller et al. (2002) from Centre for Research on the Wider Benefits of Learning). As far as I remember, I first came across the expression: 'Wider benefits of learning' in a discussion with the Welsh part of NIACE (National Institute of Adult and Continuing Education) in Brussels at a E.A.R.L.A.L.L. (European Association of Regional and Local Authorities on Lifelong Learning) in the beginning of the new Century with the Welsh Minister of Education Jane Davidson and Sue Waddington from NIACE as key-note speakers. At this meeting we discussed the importance of a broad concept of learning and a wide access to different kinds of learning sites, as empirical evidence from research on adult learning showed how people would engage in learning activities they found meaningful and often became more committed to get involved in continuous competence development after a successful learning experience perhaps in the field of liberal adult education. Though the significance of adults' participation in learning has been underscored again and again during the last decade we have, unfortunately, witnessed in several Nordic countries more tight conditions for participation in liberal adult education.

One of the additional outcomes demonstrated in the Finnish research is the motivation to learn, so vital for participation in lifelong learning. Besides the direct outcomes such as skills and competences, the paper shows how wider benefits of learning are crucial for the challenges of contemporary society such as globalization, social capital, employability, active citizenship, and health.

However, criticism also arises concerning the concept of lifelong learning. The transitions and emancipation from the narrow frames of a traditional society marked by social control and limiting conditions put new weights on the shoulders of the individual: the obligation continuously to be on the move to prevent a stand-still or worse, to be left behind. The contrast to the metaphors of a traditional society when education was a means to an end: to get a position, a place to stay until retirement, is obvious. Lifelong learning is both a possibility for individual and social development as well as a societal demand.

The research project presented by Hof and Fischer is concerned with this duality in the concept of lifelong learning as they examine individual perspectives on lifelong learning over the span of 25 years. The meanings, outcomes and benefits of lifelong learning have often been examined successfully through biographical research. The life-stories of individual learners demonstrate the significance of participation in various learning sites. But the retrospective glance and sense-making of the individual interviewee has, of course, the perspective of the context, situated in space and time, of the interview. Hof and Fischer have re-visited interviewees after a time span of 25 years. This enables them to examine the continuous process of identity work and how the meaning of educational processes change over the course of time in the "Precarious formations of lifelong learning" as the title of this fascinating research project is. The necessary negotiations of continuity and transformation appears in the individual biographies together with the human need to redeem the past - as the Canadian Philosopher Charles Taylor has put it (1989). We can see how participation in learning activities provides increasing possibilities for negotiations of meaning and coherence in the life of individuals.

The relationship between participation and motivation is an interesting issue in the theoretical discussions on learning. Participation – in various new fields of activity – may well be an important motivational factor in itself, both in the sense that there are social and other benefits related to participation in the learning process itself as Manninen shows, and in the sense that acquired new skills enable participation in new communities of practice. Biographical research informs us of the importance of meaning in connection with participation, and interviewees report a lack of motivation for participation in learning activities which do not make sense to the individual.

Thøgersen approaches motivational aspects of adult learning from a different angle as she discusses desire as response to experience. It is her ambition to rethink motivation from the point of view of a phenomenological understanding of desire in opposition to a focus on subjective needs or goals. The focus has changed from the internal drives of the subject to the interplay between the embodied person and the perceived world. Desire is seen as a creative force that produces motivation and originates as a response to an affective experience of attractive otherness. Hence, the learning situation should be actively created as a desirable environment which inspires the learner. This change of focus underscores the significance of didactics and pedagogy in the organization of the learning environment.

The following article by Willert continues the theoretical discussion through dealing with a different dimension of the concept of learning with a focus on learning transfer. He suggests a model showing structural relationships between four media through which individual and social learning processes may be channelled: languageing, experimental awareness, bodily action, and social exchange structure. Though admitting that more than one media for learning typically will be activated in natural settings, the distinctions emphasize the problems of learning transfer – illustrated by striking examples of lack of transfer between the different media – and the argumentation leads up to a proposal for a circumvention of the problems exemplified by the organization of a Master program which combines four learning arenas designed according to the different learning media: Auditorium, laboratory, practicum and reflection. Also in this paper we meet, from a different perspective, the emphasis on the learning environment and on a wide conceptualization of learning.

As learning takes place in many different settings and competences may be acquired in formal, non-formal, and informal contexts, the validation of competence has been a pervasive phenomenon over the last decade. But as Chaib and Prulovic show in their paper "Towards a Substantial Notion of Validation" there are very different definitions, strategies, and methods for validation in use. In their article the authors analyze two different processes of validation and interpret them in relation to the Swedish official definition of the contested concept. The analysis highlights the question of purpose and target group of the validation process, the understanding of the validation and procedures, and the outcomes and benefit. They demonstrate through the two cases the important difference between whether the intention is to validate and identify real competence or focus on hidden gaps of competences, and they show the difference between a focus on the individuals' needs or the needs of an actual company for competence development. The authors conclude that the diversity of interpretations of what validation stands for affects both the purpose and the methods used, and they argue against a strategy of validation as a solution to too many different problems.

In the next articles the focus is directed towards the qualifications of adult educators. Larson and Milana describe the long tradition for education and training for adults in Denmark and its development up to the present and examine how the qualification of adult educators is addressed in Danish educational policy documents. Although the policies during the last decade repeatedly stressed the need to enhance the quality in education and training competence, development for adult educators continues to be more or less absent in the overall reforms and political strategies for Danish education. The authors claim that there is a lack of acknowledgement of a need for special qualifications of those who are teaching adults in relation to competence development. It seems as if qualification in teaching children and young people are considered to be enough. One may ask whether the shift of emphasis from education to learning has diminished the focus on the educator.

Gougoulakis discusses professional quality for adult educators, now from a Swedish perspective as a member of a European group of researchers studying competences and professionalization in the field of adult and continuing education. He also notes that adult teacher training apparently is marginalized in comparison to primary and secondary teachers' training. A previous project by the same European research group, Q-ACT (Qualifying the adult educator) listed personal, social, didactical, methodological and societal and institutional competences for the adult educator. Gougoulakis concludes by characterizing the adult educator as "one who helps adults learn" and expresses the hope that further European research will broaden our understanding of what adult educators should know to facilitate adult learners' learning of good quality. An Aristotelian echo is heard when he writes: "Current concepts as lifelong learning, professionalization, qualification, validation, quality assurance, competencies etc, used in various policy documents, seem to interrelate in a specific way. They constitute a prevailing discourse – an articulated set of certain beliefs of the role of education in the making of the virtuous citizen."

Naturally, the theme of the conference Communication, Collaboration and Creativity in particular has been addressed by several papers. One of them deals with the "Framing of collaboration and its impact on creativity and innovative skills" in higher education. The preoccupation with how to organize pedagogical settings in order to facilitate creativity and emergence of new knowledge has increasingly appeared in different contexts for educational research and development during the last decade or two. The authors of this chapter, Lund and Aarup Jensen describe an experiment using a didactical tool, the KUBUS concept (developed in order to scaffold collaboration, creativity and innovation in project based work) at the master program in learning and Innovative Change at Aalborg University in Denmark. In this concept a dual management system and a differentiation between the process-oriented pre-ject (problem-finding) phase and the more goal-oriented project (problem solution) phase assist a high degree of playful and open group-climate which seems to minimize premature closings in the problem-finding process. The authors stress the importance of a space for idea generation and reduction of well known fears such as loss of face, and loss of social status within groups.

Collaboration within groups may not automatically enhance creativity. Lund and Aarup Jensen discuss the risk of premature closings in group discussions; Albrechtsen and Rüsselbæk Hansen argue that teacher teams in some cases do not lead to creative teaching but rather to more conservative teaching styles in cases where participants in the teams experience an artificial form of contrived collegiality and an experience of intensification and stress. Implementation of teacher teams as a result of a reform in the Danish upper secondary schools is supposed to enhance professionalization among the teachers and lead to creative teaching. However, the impact of external policies is not always straightforward or linear. In line with European research on the impact of teacher teams, the authors see both tendencies toward de-professionalization and re-professionalization among the teachers according to how they cope with the changes of a long tradition and culture of noninterference and the new demands. They stress the importance of the development of a new vocabulary that allows an interdisciplinary discussion on pedagogical issues that will challenge the individual teacher's beliefs.

We need, from time to time, to have our views and beliefs challenged and disturbed by different perspectives. This is one of the ways in which communication, collaboration and creativity work together as interdependent aspects of learning processes, also in research. In order to challenge habitual views from long Nordic traditions of adult education and Nordic 'group-think' we invited key-note speakers from outside to present us with very different perspectives. The last chapter in this anthology demonstrates how we as adult educators or researchers of adult learning from the Nordic countries may learn and review our own ideas and practices from the experiences of adult educators in a very different part of the world with very different circumstances. In her key-note speech, Walters told us about lifelong, life-wide and life-deep learning: utilizing the lens of HIV/AIDS in Southern Africa.

HIV/AIDS is a very serious problem in South Africa and partly responsible for a demographic profile diametrically opposite to that of the Nordic countries where the age of the population is rising. The South African population is both infected and affected by HIV/AIDS in several ways, confronted with immense social problems and senses of death, loss and trauma. Like in all other countries, the needs for adult learning programmes cross a vast economic and social spectrum, but the specific situation in South Africa highlights the fact that for many learners, attempting to create sustainable livelihoods is central to their participation in learning. Adult education in this context illustrates examples of "holistic approaches to adult learning which are 'life-wide' and 'life deep' which acknowledge the economic and systemic necessities; the personal skills required; the need participants have to belong and experience their humanness; and the need to build solidarity both with one another and also with the broader community." The South African perspective can remind us of the importance of developing methodologies "to work with the head, the hearth and the hands", and the necessity to recognize the full humanity of all people. Today, we are, also in the

Nordic countries, a population where some people have experiences of trauma or xenophobia. The view through the lens of a different context may support our self-reflections and enlighten blind spots in our Nordic approaches to adult learning and perhaps, in this way, redeem some of the ideals behind the interdependent concepts: 'communication, collaboration, and creativity'.

Marianne Horsdal
December 2010

References

EU Commission 2000. Memorandum on Lifelong Learning. EU Commission.

Gleerup, J. Forskningstilknytning og Professionsudvikling. In Gleeup, J. & Wiedemann, F. (eds.) 2002 Pædagogisk Forskning og Udvikling, Odense: Syddansk Universitetsforlag

Gleerup, J. Viden(skabs)teori. In Buur Hansen, N. & Gleerup, J. (eds.) 2004 Videnteori, Professionsuddannelse og Professionsforskning, Odense: Syddansk Universitetsforlag

Schuller, T., Brassett-Grundy, A., Green, A., Hammond, C. and Preston, J. 2002. Learning, Continuity and Change in Adult Life, Wider Benefits of Learning Research Report No. 3. Centre for Research on the Wider Benefits of Learning, London: Institute of Education

Taylor, C. 1989. Sources of the Self. The Making of Modern Identity. Cambridge: Cambridge University Pres.

Wider Benefits of Learning within the Liberal Adult Education System in Finland

Dr. Jyri Manninen

Introduction

Aim of the study

This paper is based on recent research (Manninen & Luukannel 2008) where the aim was to analyse the wider benefits of participation in liberal adult education. The general idea was to examine the wider benefits of learning person's experience as (1) an individual, (2) a citizen and (3) an employee. These three levels were selected because the intent of the study was to analyse outcomes and benefits not only from the individual perspective, but from the point of view of the community (family, workplace and neighbourhood) and society as well. The third, the work-related, perspective refers to a policy discussion where traditionally non-vocational liberal adult education institutions have also been challenged to provide vocationally oriented courses, such as ICT skills, language courses for immigrants etc. The results will therefore help to define the role and meaning of liberal adult education in society and individual life situations, as well as a work-related training system.

The paper includes an empirical part presenting the main results, and a more theoretically oriented discussion where the wider benefits of learning are related to several societal megatrends (e.g. globalisation), policy rhetoric (e.g. Lifelong learning, Active citizenship) and a number of theoretical concepts such as human and social capital. The results will show that adult learning has many wider benefits beyond the immediate learning results, and the fact that these benefits are useful not only to individuals but to communities and society in general. Adult learning, in this case liberal adult education, is therefore an important part of society and develops many skills which are considered relevant in current educational policy, for example, skills related to active citizenship.

Wider benefits approach in educational research
The study was based on the so-called wider benefits approach (see Schuller et al. 2002), where the key question is how people, groups, organisations and society benefit from education. Especially active in this field of research has been the University of London (Centre for Research on the Wider Benefits of Learning, www.learningbenefits.net), where different data and research designs have been employed to assess the impacts of educational level and educational participation.

Earlier studies (Feinstein et al. 2003; Schuller et al. 2002; Hammond 2002) have demonstrated that adult education impacts on changes in behaviour and attitudes, on several health-related issues such as social well-being and health behaviour (smoking, alcohol use) and mental well-being. Adult learning also helps adults develop communication and social skills, general skills, attitudes related to citizenship, creates a sense of group membership, and improves learning skills and learner self-image.

Education also cultivates social capital and social cohesion since participation leads to developing certain meta-competencies, such as becoming aware of the importance of active citizenship and gaining the actual skills needed in it (Schuller et al. 2002). Participation in education also helps to generate and maintain social networks, which are the building blocks of social capital (see Putnam 1995).

Data

The study is based on the experiences of adult learners who participated in study groups offered by liberal adult education organisations (adult education centres, folk high schools, summer universities, study centres and physical education centres) in Finland in 2007. In Finland in 2005 a total of 1,066,932 adults participated in these groups. The contents and aims of these liberal studies is not dictated by the state, even though in 2008 it financed the system through a budget of 192 million euro.

The data was collected using theme interviews (n = 19 adult learners), focus group (Morgan 1998) interviews (12 study groups, 77 adult learners) and a survey (n = 1744 adult learners). The data is therefore both qualitative and quantitative. Interview data and open-ended questions in the survey were analysed using qualitative content analysis. Structured questions in the survey were explored using statistical analysis (factor analysis).

The majority (66 %) of the adult learners in this study participated in courses offered by adult education centres. The second largest group (14 %) studied at study centres and 12 % at summer university. Respondents were mostly women (76 %), and half of them were working full time; the second largest group consisted of retired people (29 %). More than one third of the participants (37 %) were in the age group of 50 – 63 years old. These numbers reflect the actual participation structures (see Kumpulainen 2007) quite well.

Qualitative data and analysis
The qualitative data include theme interviews, focus group interviews and open-ended answers in the survey. The key questions in the interviews and the open-ended questions were

(1) what direct benefits has the learning provided,
(2) what wider benefits have there been, and
(3) what other outcomes have there been in your life?

The data were inspected through open-ended qualitative content analysis, where different themes were identified from the data. An example from individual interviews is given below.

Table 1. Example of analysis (individual interview)

	What direct benefits have there been?	What wider benefits of learning have you had?
Work related benefits	None directly, but Spanish is the only Romance language I have studied. **Now I can understand some French and Italian.** Sometimes there are documents, and then **language skills are useful in my work.**	A wider benefit is that I **have some knowledge about Romance languages.** In my former job there were, for example, some papers in French, which **I was somehow able to read.**
As an individual?	It has been useful, **I can discuss things in Spanish.** I have been to Spain and Venezuela, and my **language skills were useful.** Developing language skills is **important** and **fun.**	A wider benefit is that **I have a knowledge of Romance languages, which is useful.** I better **understand** Spanish and even Portuguese texts. I had a few years' break in my studies and it's **good to see that I am still able to learn** languages. There's also **a feeling that I can develop** in that area.
As a citizen?	Earlier I used to work in a voluntary organisation where **language skills were useful** and related to my tasks and role as an active citizen. At the moment I have no direct use for Spanish as an active citizen.	None.

Several themes begin to evolve from this data example, such as language skills, joy of learning, self confidence and learner self image, and learning motivation.

Different data sources (individual and group interviews and open-ended answers) provided identical results. The main analysis is therefore based on a more detailed content analysis of the open-ended answers (n = 1744 adult learners), which at the same time makes possible an empirically sound qualitative analysis as well as representative and transferable (Lincoln & Guba 1985) results based on a larger number of respondents. Here we combine qualitative, open-ended content analysis with a more structured quantification procedure (Silverman 1993), where the frequency of a theme mentioned in the data is calculated.

The qualitative analysis of open-ended answers was based on the responses of 1744 adult learners to three questions (what direct benefits has learning provided, what wider benefits have there been, and what other outcomes have there been in your life). A total of 2521 individual statements (such as *"new language skills have made it possible to travel and communicate with local people"*) were identified from the data. These were placed under 35 main themes (such as "internationalisation skills"). The main themes were subsequently positioned in five categories (such as "Skills & competences"). An example is given below.

Table 2. Example of analysis (open-ended answers, n = 1744)

Example of individual answer	Statements (f=2521)	Main themes (35)
Everything has been educational, fun, uplifting and given me new inspiration. New language skills have made it possible to travel and communicate with local people.	Everything has been educational	General knowledge
	fun	Joy of learning
	uplifting and given me new inspiration	New inspiration
	New language skills have made it possible to travel and communicate with local people.	Internationalisation skills

As the number of respondents and answers was high (1744 respondents and three main open-ended questions, which generated 5232 individual answers), the so-called saturation principle was used in the analysis. Consequently, answers to each question were analysed so long as the analysis provided (a) new main themes and (b) each additional 100 answers changed the percentage of the individual main themes by more than

1 %. For example, the analysis of the first question (what direct benefits has learning provided) reached a saturation point at 1000 answers, which included 1310 statements. The saturation point for the other questions was 703 answers (762 statements) and 606 answers (449 statements), respectively. The ratio between number of answers (respondents) and statements varies because (1) there are some empty answers, and (2) some included several statements, some only one.

Quantification of main themes made it possible to identify the themes (outcomes, benefits of learning) which were mentioned more often in the data. For example, the main theme "internationalisation skills" (language skills, cultural awareness) was mentioned 192 times, which means that 19.2 % of respondents had mentioned it as an outcome. Of the statements (f= 2521), 14.7 % are part of this main theme. "Joy of learning", on the other hand, was mentioned 56 times, which means that 5.6 % of the respondents mentioned outcomes included in this main theme.

The complete table of results is presented in Appendix 1 and the results in model form later in this paper.

Credibility and transferability of results
According to Lincoln & Guba (1985; also Silverman 1993) the traditional positivist measures of validity and reliability should be replaced by other criteria in qualitative research. Instead of internal validity, they suggest assessing the credibility of results, which basically means that "the reconstructions of the researcher correspond to the constructions of the informants". In plain language, this means that the results describe the experiences and conceptions of the respondents. In this study the qualitative analysis was data-driven, in other words, the main themes were defined and named using the original statements and language.

External validity should be evaluated by asking how transferable the results are. In qualitative research the results are usually transferable only to situations and settings similar to those where the data were collected. The research process should be described in such detail that the readers are able to assess the transferability of the results in other populations and cultures. Since the results of this study are almost identical to those of earlier studies (e.g. Schuller et al. 2002; Dehrman & Stacey 1997; Feinstein et al. 2003), it seems fair to assume that the results have some wider relevance as well, even though they undeniably reveal many cultural and contextual differences.

Rather than reliability, we should assess the dependability of the results. It is often unrealistic to assume that in behavioural sciences the results remain unaltered in the course of time since the phenomena themsleves are constantly changing, and there are so many intervening variables. Instead, we should assess how the data collection situation has influenced the results. In this study data triangulation (individual and group interviews and open-ended questions in the survey) provided identical results and it is, therefore, fair to assume that the results have some stability over time.

Wider benefits of learning

The main results of the study are presented in this section. They are primarily based on the qualitative data (interviews, open-ended answers), but some key observations from the statistical data are also presented. Such "hard evidence" is usually considered by decision-makers as the "only" evidence. In this study it provides "another" perspective on the phenomena, since the survey results and those of the qualitative content analysis are basically similar and therefore mutually supportive. The qualitative analysis tends to provide a conceptual map or field of the wider benefits of learning (i.e. what are the benefits?), and the quantitative analysis shows the "depth" or "strength" of the benefits in the wider population (i.e. how many people have experienced these benefits and how strong has the impact been?).

Conceptual model of wider benefits of learning
The following model summarises the qualitative results, which are described in detail in Appendix 1. The boxes indicate five categories, in which the 35 main themes are listed in order of frequency. For example, in the category "Further benefits" the main theme of "mental well-being" was mentioned by 28 % of the respondents, but "participation in society" by only 2.6 %.

These percentages should not be misinterpreted as indicating "how many have experienced" benefits of this kind, because they only reveal "how many have spontaneously mentioned" this particular benefit in their open-ended answers. It is likely that many more than 28 % of adult learners experienced outcomes and benefits which help to maintain good mental health, but for one reason or another do not mention it spontaneously. The statistical data, on the contrary, facilitates the analysis of how many respondents gained at least some benefit from each main theme.

Figure 1. Conceptual model of wider benefits of learning

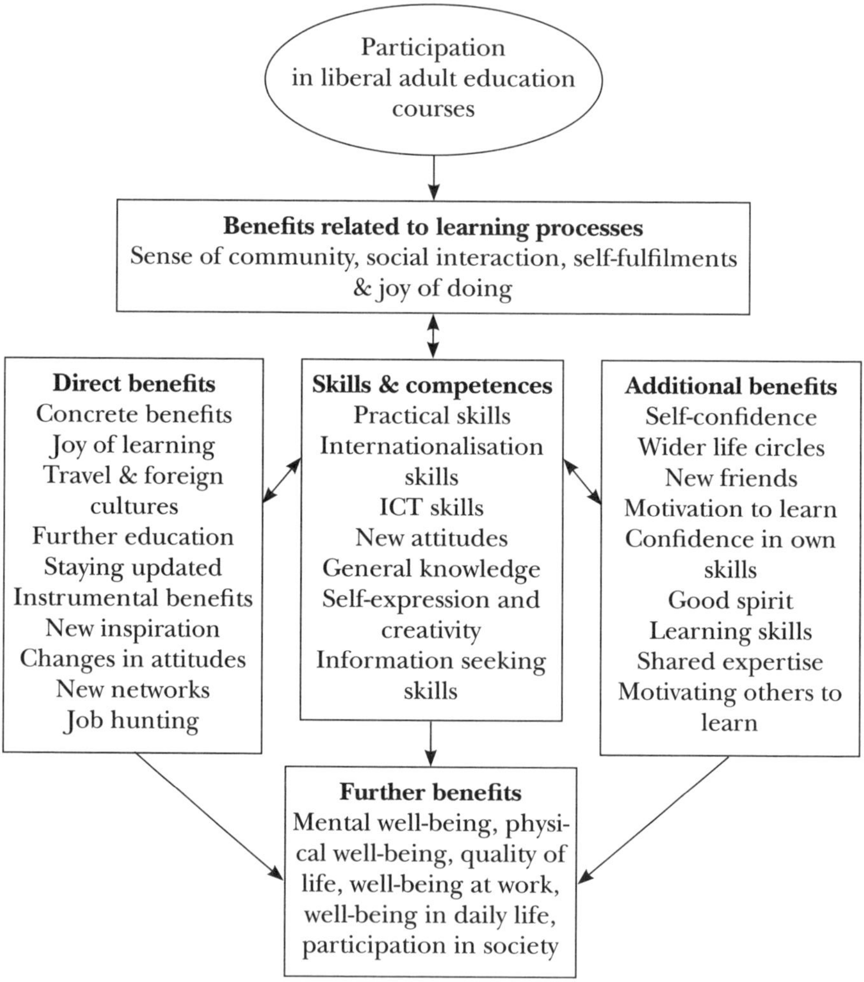

```
                    ┌─────────────────────┐
                    │    Participation    │
                    │ in liberal adult    │
                    │  education courses  │
                    └──────────┬──────────┘
                               ▼
        ┌──────────────────────────────────────────────┐
        │     Benefits related to learning processes   │
        │ Sense of community, social interaction,      │
        │      self-fulfilments & joy of doing         │
        └──────────────────────────────────────────────┘
```

Direct benefits	Skills & competences	Additional benefits
Concrete benefits	Practical skills	Self-confidence
Joy of learning	Internationalisation skills	Wider life circles
Travel & foreign cultures	ICT skills	New friends
Further education	New attitudes	Motivation to learn
Staying updated	General knowledge	Confidence in own skills
Instrumental benefits	Self-expression and creativity	Good spirit
New inspiration	Information seeking skills	Learning skills
Changes in attitudes		Shared expertise
New networks		Motivating others to learn
Job hunting		

Further benefits
Mental well-being, physical well-being, quality of life, well-being at work, well-being in daily life, participation in society

The model is based on the assumption that the learning outcomes and wider benefits have some kind of causal path, which is indicated using arrows between the boxes. There are some **benefits which are directly related to learning processes**, such as having a sense of community, "feelings of belonging to some group". The usual outcome of learning is the **development of skills and competencies**, for example, language skills. There are usually **direct benefits** from learning these skills as well, for instance, new language skills can make it easier to travel and become familiar with foreign cultures. In the long run this may lead to **additional benefits**, for example, wider life circles, better self-confidence and new friends. All these may eventually raise the quality of life, well-being at work and daily life etc., which we refer to here as **further benefits** of learning.

The following examples from the data help to assess the credibility of the model. The first example shows how participation and its wider benefits form a "causal" path:

> "When I started in the poem circle, I had just moved into the village as a new resident. The group welcomed me very cordially, which made it easier to create other social contacts in the village. Learning new presentation skills and gaining new contacts have helped and motivated me to join other local societies as well". (#439, woman born in 1967, culture producer, adult education centre)

The data provide strong empirical evidence that adult learning has an influence on mental as well as physical well-being, as the following example shows:

> "Joint actions of people who have similar values and common objectives help me to feel better both mentally and physically. At home I am able to make use of the skills I have learned on the course". (#471, woman born in 1943, retired, adult education centre)

Schuller et al. (2002, 6) report that in their literature survey they found little evidence of education directly improving physical health; the only exceptions were some older people. On the other hand, the mental health effects were clear, and it is fair to assume that adult education plays an important but unrecognized role in national health systems. In this study, in the qualitative data, 28 % of the respondents spontaneously cited mental well-being as an outcome of learning, and 13.2 % mentioned improved physical health. In the statistical analysis 62 % indicated that participation has, at least to some degree, helped to maintain their physical health. The figure for mental well-being was 95 %.

"Hard evidence"

The quantitative data and results of this study are based on the survey (n = 1744). Adult learners were asked to assess their learning outcomes by means of a list of potential effects which were defined using the preliminary results of the individual and focus group interviews in this study, and the results of earlier studies (Hammond 2002; Schuller et al. 2002; Dehrman & Stacey 1997; Feinstein et al. 2003). Structured questions under the heading "How much has your participation had an impact on the following factors…" were assessed on a scale of 1-5 (not at all – a lot).

Factor analysis suggested that the outcomes and benefits of learning can be summarised in five factors (Active citizenship, Well-being, Skills & competencies, Work & income, Learning motivation) as summarised in Table 3.

The first factor was named "Active citizenship", since the variables loading it were clearly skills and competencies necessary in any active role within the local community, network or society in general. A sense of responsibility and self-confidence are the starting points for active participation, and social skills together with networks facilitate it.

Table 3. Results of the factor analysis (n = 1744

Active citizenship	Well-being	Skills & competencies	Work & income	Learning motivation
Sense of responsibility Societal involvement Social skills Social networks Critical thinking Self-confidence	Endurance Physical health Mental health Creativity Self-esteem	Knowledge Skills General knowledge	Earning opportunities Career development	Learning motivation

In a similar way the factors "Well-being", "Skills & competencies" and "Work & income" were easy to identify. "Learning motivation" is based on a single variable, which was removed from the final analysis because it loaded too strongly on all factors. The basic reason for this is that almost all respondents indicated that their participation in liberal adult education courses had an impact on learning motivation.

Variables contained in each factor were used to create a sum score. This statistical analysis made it possible to define how strongly adult learners experienced the benefits of participation in each category. The most signficant result is summarised in Figure 2. It shows that participation in liberal adult education has **at least some influence** on learning motivation (93 %), development of skills and competencies (84 %), well-being (88 %), and skills needed in active citizenship (81 %).

It seems that liberal adult education has less impact on skills which are related to work and income; only 33 % of the respondents feel that participation had at least some impact on this area, and the majority (67 %) experienced no work-related benefits at all. This result should, however, be assessed in the light of the fact that by definition liberal adult education is non-vocational. Only 2.3 % of the courses in our data had a direct vocational orientation (e.g. the basic degree for tourist guides organised by a local adult education centre), and only 4.8 % was otherwise related to work (e.g. accounting for labour union administration). It is therefore obvious that learning general, non-work related skills can be beneficial in work as well, for example, in developing new social networks. The following statement from the open-ended answers describes this:

> "We have been in contact with other participants after the course, and we have helped each other in problematic situations. At the same time my own skills are developing and I can be more useful at my own workplace as well". (#1544, man born in 1970, car mechanic, studied at folk high school on a labour union course)

Figure 2. How much impact has participation had on the following factors...
(n = 1744)

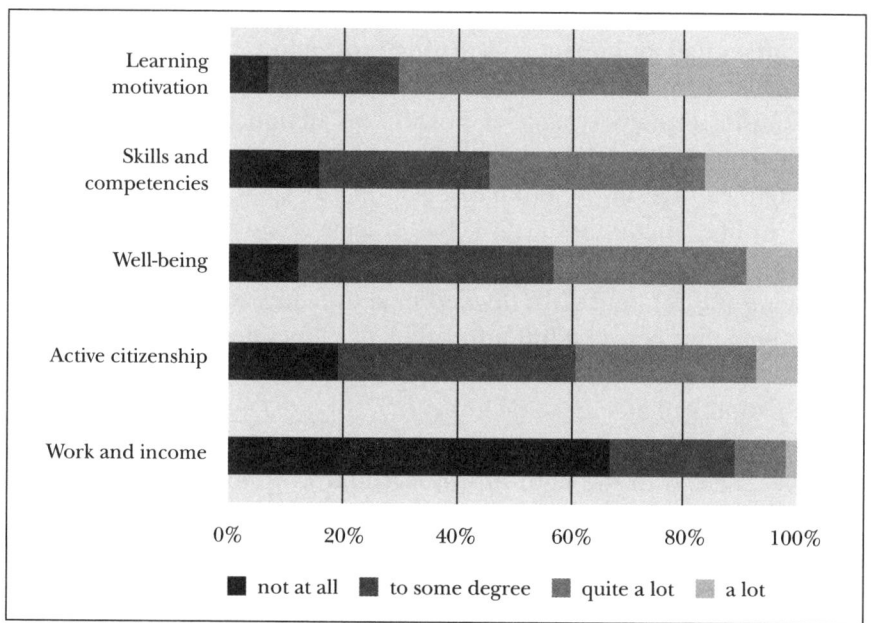

Discussion

The results of this study are similar to those of earlier ones (Hammond 2002; Schuller et al. 2002; Dehrman & Stacey 1997; Feinstein et al. 2003; Riihimäki & Saarenpää-Numminen 2005; Kansalaisopistotoiminnan vaikuttavuus 2001), and it is therefore fair to assume that liberal adult education has many positive outcomes and benefits in peoples' lives. There are also outcomes which benefit – at least in a long run – wider communities and society in general. Some of these benefits are discussed in more detail below.

Meaning of liberal adult education in society

Finland has a population of five million. According to statistics (Kumpulainen 2007) a total of 1,066,932 adults participated in liberal adult education in 2005. In this study 93 % of the respondents state that participation has motivated them to learn more. Assuming that the results are transferable to whole population, it is possible to estimate that 992,247

Finns now have, at least to some degree, increased their learning motivation as a result of participating in liberal adult education (see Table 4). This result indicates that the liberal adult education system plays an important role in the learning society, because the motivation to learn is the basic requisite for lifelong learning. Another important outcome is self-confidence, which plays a central role in the theories of participation (for literature reviews, see Manninen & Birke 2005; Manninen 1996)

In a similar way, we can estimate that approximately 900,000 people have been able to develop their skills and competencies, well-being, and skills related to active citizenship. Even work-related skills and income possibilities have improved for 352,000 people, although these items are not among the main objectives in liberal studies.

Table 4. Benefits of liberal adult education adjusted for participation rates

Benefits	Percentage of respondents (n=1744) who felt at least some improvement in this area	Impact, adjusted for total number of participants (1,066,932)
Learning motivation	93%	992,247 persons
Skills & competencies	84%	896,223 persons
Well-being	88%	938,900 persons
Active citizenship	81%	864,215 persons
Work & income	33%	352,088 persons

Liberal education as a policy tool
The Lisbon strategy set the modest target that by 2010 the EU would be the leading learning society in the world. There are still a few months left to reach this target. European neoliberal training policy is clearly based on lifelong learning as *The Tool* for economic development and global competitiveness. In 2000, the Commission published a memorandum on lifelong learning stating that "access to up-to-date information and knowledge […] are becoming the key to strengthening Europe's

competitiveness and improving the employability and adaptability of the workforce". (EU Commission 2000)

In a similar way OECD points out that "the renewal of knowledge and skills is increasingly a prerequisite for meeting basic needs, for participation in economic activities, and more broadly for full and active citizenship" (OECD 2005). Therefore it is no surprise that Longworth & Davies (1996, 64) suggest that "Lifelong Learning has become a synonym for Lifelong Earning and Lifelong Employability".

The proposed benchmark for adult participation in lifelong learning for 2010 is that at least 12.5 % of adults (aged 25-64) should participate in this activity. Lifelong learning is computed here on the basis of "participation in education and training in the last four weeks". The lowest rate (1.3 %) was found in Romania and Bulgaria. In 2007 the EU average was 9.5 % and was falling rather than rising (2005: 9.8 % and 2006: 9.7 %). Only the Nordic countries had better participation rates: for example, Finland 23.4 % and Sweden 32.4 % in 2007 (EU Commission 2009).

Visions and policy seem to be clearly contradicted by the current reality. In practice lifelong learning is a luxury only those with a higher educational level can enjoy, because there is an imbalance in participation between poorly and highly skilled adults. The reality in European workplaces is rather different than in policy documents: 57 % of poorly skilled adults have simple jobs which take only a few hours to learn, and 64 % have poor advancement opportunities in their jobs (Manninen & Birke 2005).

The adult learners in this study participated in liberal adult education, which by nature has chiefly non-vocational objectives. The reasons for participating in their studies were mainly learning-oriented and social (Houle 1961), and only 21 % had strong work-related motives. It seems that these adult learners still live according to the "old lifelong learning" model and values, which was based on personal growth and humanistic ideals (see Faure 1972), instead of the current economy-driven competitiveness and employability objectives.

However, policy-makers should not despair. Empirical evidence in this paper shows that many of the policy objectives are actualized when adults participate in liberal adult education. Many current policy-related "buzz words" become relevant when we take a deeper look at the outcomes of learning. Some of these buzz words are based on megatrends (such as globalisation and aging workforce), some on EU policy (Lifelong learning, Active citizenship), and some have a more theoretical origin, for example, in sociology (Social capital).

A theoretically interesting point of view is the concept of social capital, which originates in Bourdieu (1986). He saw economic, cultural and social capital as the building blocks of social class. Putnam (1995) later defined social capital to consist of moral obligations and norms, social values (especially trust) and existing social networks. Putnam places particular emphasis on participation in voluntary associations.

Participation in liberal adult education seems to directly support these policy objectives and provide tools for facing other challenges, such as globalisation (see Table 5). For example, the development of a "Sense of community" and skills related to "Societal involvement" are likely to support so-called **active citizenship**. Moreover, **Social capital** (Putnam 1995) is stronger if people have "Networks" and "Self-confidence". In a similar way "Learning motivation", "Confidence in own skills", "Joy of learning" and development of "Learning skills" are all important parts of **lifelong learning**.

Table 5. Wider benefits of learning and societal challenges

Challenges	What people get from liberal AE?
Globalization	Language skills, Cultural competencies
Active citizenship	Sense of community, Societal involvement
Social capital	Networks, Self-confidence
Lifelong learning	Learning motivation, Confidence in own skills, Joy of learning, Learning skills
Employability	Practical skills, ICT skills, General knowledge, Well-being at work
Health	Physical well-being
Mental health	Mental well-being, Well-being at work & daily life, Life quality

Social capital has been quite widely used in literature when outcomes and wider benefits of learning are discussed. For example Schuller et al. (2002) analyse their results using the concepts of social and human capital and social cohesion. In the Finnish literature social capital has been discussed, for example, from the standpoint of health (Hyyppä 2004) and work organisations (Koivumäki 2008). Related concepts are human capital, cultural capital and intellectual capital. Human capital, for example, is defined as knowledge, skills and qualifications that individuals acquire during learning processes, and is therefore more often related to outcomes of education.

Social capital is based (according to Putnam 1995) on social networks, trust, norms and cooperation, and is therefore not an individual characteristic but a social one, belonging to groups of people. In this study one of the learning benefits was the creation and development of social networks. Schuller et al. (2002) have also reported that an additional benefit of learning was a strengthening of social networks (individuals' entry into new networks, extension of existing networks, and the restoration of old networks).

Social capital and social cohesion are also related to Active citizenship, which requires some networking possibilities as well as skills. In this study these skills were, for example, self-confidence and new networks, which facilitate societal involvement and participation in society. Schuller et al. (2002) reported similar results and defined them as "metacompetences", "generic skills", and "basic competences", which they saw as "necessary for anyone to fulfil minimum citizenship requirements" (Schuller et al. 2002, 7).

References

Behrman, J. & Stacey, N. 1997. The Social Benefits of Education. Ann Arbor: University of Michigan Press.

Bourdieu, P. 1986. The forms of capital. In: John G. Richardson (ed.): Handbook of Theory and Research for the Sociology of Education. New York: Greenwood Press.

EU Commission 2000. Memorandum on Lifelong Learning. EU Commission.

EU Commission, Directorate-General for Education and Culture 2009. Directorate A: Lifelong learning: horizontal Lisbon policy issues and international affairs, EAC A4 - Analysis and studies. 2009. Benchmarks – sheets 20.2.2009. EU Commission.

Faure, E. et al., 1972. Learning to be. Paris: Unesco.
Feinstein, L., Hammond, C., Woods, L., Preston, J. & Bynner, J. 2003. The contribution of adult learning to health and social capital. Wider Benefits of Learning Research Report No. 8. London: Institute of Education.
Hammond, C. 2002. What is it about education that makes us healthy? Exploring the education-health connection. International Journal of Lifelong Education, 21(06), pp.551-571.
Houle, C. O. 1961. The inquiring mind. Madison, WI: University of Wisconsin Press.
Hyyppä, M. 2004. Kertyykö sosiaalisesta pääomasta kansanterveyttä? Yhteiskuntapolitiikka. 2004:4. Stakes. Helsinki. s. 380–386
Kansalaisopistotoiminnan vaikuttavuus 2001. Kaiku-projektin I osa. Tampere: Tampereen työväenopisto.
Koivumäki, J. 2008. Työyhteisöjen sosiaalinen pääoma. Tutkimus luottamuksen ja yhteisöllisyyden rakentumisesta ja merkityksestä muuttuvissa valtion asiantuntijaorganisaatioissa. Tampereen yliopisto. Tampere.
Kumpulainen, T. (ed.) 2007. Aikuiskoulutuksen vuosikirja. Tilastotietoja aikuisten opiskelusta 2005. Opetusministeriön julkaisuja 2007:26
Lincoln & Guba 1985. Naturalistic inquiry. Beverly Hills: Sage.
Longworth, N. & Davies, W. K. 1996. Lifelong learning. London: Kogan Page.
Manninen, J. 2006. Development of participation models. From single predicting elements to modern interpretation. In: Participation in Adult Education. Theory, research, practice. Mechelen: ERDI Consortium of European Research and Development Institutes for Adult Education.
Manninen, J. & Birke, B. 2005 (eds.) Lifelong Learning and European reality - learning motivation of lower qualified workers. Qualitative study in eight European countries. Pdf: www.motivation-LLL.net.
Manninen, J. & Luukannel, S. 2008. Omaehtoisen aikuisopiskelun vaikutukset. Vapaan sivistystyön opintojen merkitys ja vaikutukset aikuisten elämässä. Helsinki: VSY.
Morgan, D. L. 1998. The focus group guidebook. Focus Group Kit 1. Thousand Oaks, CA: Sage.
OECD 2005. Beyond rhetoric: Adult learning policies and practices, the final report of the OECD thematic review on adult learning. http://www.oecd.org/els/education/adultlearning.
Putnam, R. 1995. Bowling alone: The collapse and revival of American community. Journal of Democracy Vol. 6 (1995) 1, 64-78.
Riihimäki, K. & Saarenpää-Numminen, M. 2005. Kansalaisopisto – kulttuuria

ja elämälaatua kuntaan. Hämeenkyrö: Kansalaistoiminnan kulttuuriyhteisöllinen vaikuttavuus–hanke.

Schuller, T., Brassett-Grundy, A., Green, A., Hammond, C. and Preston, J. 2002. Learning, Continuity and Change in Adult Life, Wider Benefits of Learning Research Report No. 3. Centre for Research on the Wider Benefits of Learning. London: Institute of Education.

Silverman, D. 1993. Interpreting qualitative data. Methods for analysing talk, text and interaction. London: Sage.

Appendix

Main results from qualitative content analysis (open answers, n of respondents 1744, n of answers 606 - 1000)

% of respondents	% of statements	n of statements	Main themes and subcategories
			Skills & competences
33.7	25.7	337	Practical skills
19.2	14.7	192	Internationalisation skills
14.2	10.8	142	ICT skills
11.7	12.4	79	New attitudes
7.8	6.0	78	General knowledge
1.1	0.8	11	Self-expression and creativity
1.0	0.8	10	Information-seeking skills
			Direct benefits
20.4	21.8	137	Concrete benefits
5.6	4.3	56	Joy of learning
7.7	8.2	52	Travel & foreign cultures
3.5	2.7	35	Further education
4.5	4.8	30	Staying updated
3.5	3.7	23	Instrumental benefits
2.1	1.6	21	New inspiration

1.6	1.2	16	Change of attitudes
1.4	1.1	14	New networks
0.7	0.5	7	Job hunting
			Benefits related to learning processes
21.6	23.7	143	Sense of community
2.4	1.8	24	Social interaction
12.5	4.2	24	Self-fulfilment & joy of doing
			Additional benefits
15.1	14.7	119	Self-confidence
18.0	21.6	115	Wider life circles
15.4	18.7	98	New friends
11.6	12.7	77	Motivation to learn
3.4	3.7	23	Confidence on own skills
2.0	1.5	20	Good spirit
2.4	2.3	17	Learning skills
2.3	2.4	16	Shared expertise
1.2	1.4	8	Motivating others to learn
			Further benefits
28.0	27.0	214	Mental well-being
13.2	11.5	117	Physical well-being
14.7	14.3	113	Quality of life
8.6	8.2	69	Well-being at work
5.3	5.5	36	Well-being in daily life
2.6	2.0	26	Participation in society
			Total number of statements: 2499

Lifelong Learning as Continuity and Transformation. A Qualitative Longitudinal Study of Adults' Biographies of Learning

Hof, C./Fischer, M. E.

1. Introduction

Until the 1980s the catchword "Modernity" was associated with the hope of relief from coercive traditions, and the extensive assertion of an individual emancipation from social restraints (cf. Beck/Bonß 2001, Beck/Giddens/Lash 1996). Modern individuals were supposed to decide for themselves who they were and who they wanted to be. This claim to self-determination was however accompanied by the expectation that individuals should actively contribute to their own self-realization (cf. Beck/Lau 2004). According to the logic of modernity, self-determination and self-realization appeared to be attainable and desirable aims (cf. Fischer-Rosenthal 2005).

In the meantime modernity's enthusiastic hopes for the implementation of increased social control as well as the exuberant belief in progress have given way to more sceptical estimations of the future. Modernity today is therefore perceived to be much more ambivalent. Besides chance, risk has now also been acknowledged as an essential feature of modernity:

- The transition from a largely static society to a dynamic society is no longer perceived solely in terms of the chances this transformation offers for individuals to choose their place in society, but also in terms of the risk of increased social fragmentation and possible precarity.
- The disembedding of social relationships from time and space and their readjustment over extensive spans of time and space are no longer exclusively found to offer the individual greater freedom of choice in social relationships: they are henceforth also regarded as

conditions that lead to a constant requirement to make decisions concerning social relationships, which involves the actualization as well as the negation of competing relationships.
– The course of an individual's life is no longer determined largely by social background. Indeed, the course of an individual's life is increasingly plastic, thanks to the possibility of individualized decisions. This is no longer described solely as the subject's deliverance from traditional bonds, but also as the loss of formerly existing securities (cf. Alheit 2009, Alheit/Dausein 2002, Beck/Beck-Gernsheim 1994, Fischer 2007).

To this day, the as yet unclouded hopes of liberation and emancipation associated with modernity can be found in the discourse about Lifelong Learning. This concept emerged in the early 1970s (cf. Hof 2009) and describes a special form of education in modern societies. The Faure-Report (Faure et al. 1972) marks a change of perspective in our understanding of education, establishing a new understanding of the interrelationship between the individual and education. Education is no longer conceptualized as something that is externally imposed on individuals, but depicted – in the form of Lifelong Learning – as something that discloses superior and more individualized opportunities to assimilate and adopt knowledge than ever before. This way education is conceptualized as a means of lifelong self-development in all areas of life instead of being declared an artifact of social control. This understanding of learning as a lifelong process affecting all spheres of life implies the necessity of a continuous and never-ending education.

The concept of Lifelong Learning also sets itself apart from other concepts of education as activities of learning are no longer understood to be temporary insertions in the course of a life. Learning is understood as an integral part of everyday life (cf. Brödel 2009, Commission of the European Communities 2000, Hof 2009, Kade/Seitter 2007). Lifelong Learning centers on the individual when it comes to reflection on learning. As someone considered capable of making decisions, the individual is also expected to make decisions when it comes to participation in formal, non-formal and informal education.

At the same time the individual's learning seems to be compatible with the demands society imposes on individuals. The individual's learning and hence the individual's progression – even in its subversive forms

– seem to be a fundamental part of collective advancement. This is true for conservative learning, which links up to things already established, as well as for evolutionary-experimental learning, the usefulness of which is still to be proven (cf. Commission of the European Communities 2000, Kade/Seitter 2007). Unlike many other concepts of education, Lifelong Learning therefore complies with the paradigms of modernity – individualization and progression.

Recently there has been more and more criticism of the concept of Lifelong Learning.

Lifelong Learning is no longer perceived as an unfettered chance enabling self-determining individuals to promote their own perfection. Some also see Lifelong Learning as a risky programme with totalitarian claims, one which permanently enforces learning as a socially observable achievement of individual, without there being any guarantee of its future usability (cf. Alheit 2009, Coffield 1999, Forneck 2001 Kade/Seitter 2003). The belief that Lifelong Learning ensures progression thus becomes dubious.

Empirically speaking, it is possible to observe not only successful use of Lifelong Learning, but also resistance to permanent learning and subversive forms of use such as explicit rejection, limited use, subjection of learning to aspects of everyday life such as sociability and entertainment (cf. Bolder/Hendrich 2000, Herzberg 2004, Kade 1991/1997, Kade/Seitter 1996/1998). From the biographical research point of view, Lifelong Learning therefore appears to be a field that opens up chances as well as risks, and one that is characterized by specific liberties as well as specific restrictions (Kade 1997, Kade/Seitter 1996/1998).

The research project presented in this paper is concerned with this grey area of Lifelong Learning and examines the individual's perspective on Lifelong Learning over the time span of 25 years.

Below we want to provide an insight into the research project "Precarious Formations of Lifelong Learning".[1] For that purpose we will

---

1 The research project (KA 642/4-1) (German title: "Prekäre Kontinuitäten. Der Wandel von Bildungsgestalten im großstädtischen Raum unter den Bedingungen der forcierten Durchsetzung des Lebenslangen Lernens" is lead by Prof. Dr. Jochen Kade (Goethe-Universität Frankfurt/Main) and Prof. Dr. Christiane Hof (Universität Flensburg). Further staff members are: Dr. Cornelia Maier-Gutheil, Dipl. Päd. Monika Fischer, Dipl. Päd. Sascha Benedetti, Heike Breckle, Marco Dobel.

present our main research interest. We will then outline the empirical design of the project as well as the theoretical focus. In conclusion we will give an example to illustrate the first findings of the project. These findings point out that, contrary to the common discourse on Lifelong Learning, which conceptualizes Lifelong Learning primarily as a means of enhancement and progression (cf. Alheit 2009), other phenomena prevail: the examination of individual processes of Lifelong Learning over a time span of more than 20 years discloses not only phenomena of progression, expansion and enhancement, but also phenomena of stagnation, contraction and degradation (cf. Kade/Hof 2007, p.15).

2. The Project "Precarious Formations of Lifelong Learning"

2.1. The project's main research interest

The DFG-promoted research project "Precarious Formations of Lifelong Learning" intends to explore the change of individual educational formations over nearly a quarter of a century of biographical and historical time. The project aims to provide an insight into the practice of Lifelong Learning over the course of an individual's life.

Within the scope of recent social developments (cf. Beck/Giddens/Lash 1996) individuals are – more than ever before – expected to adjust themselves continuously to the changing conditions of modern society via learning and unlearning. The uncertainty of the future, which is becoming more and more manifest, brings two major problems for individuals:

The disembedding of individuals from social ties leads to the problem that individuals must now solve the problem of their reembedding within social contexts all on their own, and over and over again. In the course of this social disembedding, the individuals' relationship with their own past, present and future becomes fragile and therefore subject to permanent change as well. In this respect one might speak of a social disembedding just as well as of a biographical disembedding, which requires the individuals to constantly readjust their positioning in social time and social space. The prevailing concept of "identity", which is still a main concept in biographical research, is no longer adequate for describing the new challenges which individuals have to confront (cf. Alheit/Dausien 2002).

The modern individual can therefore hardly be described using static concepts, since modern "identities" have become fluid: "A straightforward 'identity', in the sense of being able to identify one's self as 'This-is-who-I-am-and-this-is-who-I–am-not', is hopelessly inadequate. Identity is decentered. [...]. The answer to the question 'who am I' can be continued indefinitely, depending upon the number of situations in which it arises." (Fischer-Rosenthal 1995, p. 216).

The question "how do people cope with the problems of modernity [...]. How do they sustain a coherent social order and an integrated self?" (Fischer-Rosenthal 1995, p. 219) can thus only be answered by conceptualizing individual biographies as punctual imprints of a lifelong educational process and by comparing several of these imprints with each other (cf. Kade/Hof/Peterhoff 2008).

Based on this, our main research interest is whether and how individuals integrate their manifold experience of life and Lifelong Learning – as continuities or transformations - into a coherent biographical account of their lifetime and educational development at two different points in time.

2.2. The Project's Empirical Design

We aim to access the continuities and transformations of processes of Lifelong Learning. The project's starting point is a sample of 85 semi-structured interviews that were conducted from 1983 to 1985. The interviewees were course-instructors (n=40) and course-attendees (n=44) at different adult-education centers (German: "Volkshochschule") in an urban region in southern Germany.

The main focus of the interviews back then was the interviewee's experience in instruction and learning, especially relating to their activities at the adult-education centers.[2]

The recent project "Precarious Formations of Lifelong Learning" (cf. Hof/Kade 2009, Kade/Hof 2007/2009, Kade/Hof Peterhoff 2008) intended to examine how educational processes change over the course of time. Therefore the project tried to interview the persons who had already been interviewed around 1984 for a second time – 25 years later – on the subject of instruction and learning. This new set of interviews

---

[2] An overview and analyses of these interviews can already be found in different studies (cf. Kade 1989/1991).

places a stronger emphasis on processes of non-formal and informal learning. By interviewing the same persons twice within the course of their life, the project is able to look at the individual's educational process from two different points in time, thus combining two different perspectives on the matter. This multi-perspective approach hopefully enables us to provide an insight into the continuities and transformations of Lifelong Learning.

The research project is designed as a longitudinal study, based on recurrent interviews. This means that we do not produce statistically representative results. Instead the project generates explorative insights into the structures of change that underlie the educational processes of adults within the last 25 years.

25 years is quite a long time in the course of an individual's life. Since a second wave of interviews was not planned when the first wave was conducted, finding the former interviewees became a major challenge for the project. After painstaking research, the project was able to track down over 70 persons from the original sample. Of these 70 people, over a third had died in the past 25 years. Nonetheless, we have managed to conduct about 30 interviews for a second time. Further interviews are planned.

The project's method of choice is the Documentary Method (cf. Nohl 2006), which itself follows the principles of qualitative social research (cf. Strauss/Corbin 1996). The Documentary Method differentiates especially between the descriptive interpretation (What is said?) and the reflective interpretation (How is it said?). Particular emphasis is also put on comparisons between different pieces of research material. Only by comparing distinct fragments of the empirical reality that the project can access through the interviews are we able to reconstruct specific distinctions within the material. The categories for comparisons as well as the categories for distinctions are obtained from the research material. Detailed biographical case studies and systematic comparisons between the two interviews with one individual over the time span of 25 years, between distinct interviews with different persons over the two time periods (the 1980s and the 2000s), or between interviews with persons belonging to different generations, enable the project to generate well-grounded hypotheses about changes in learning over the course of a life.

2.3. The Project's Theoretical Focus: Formations of Lifelong Learning

The Research Project represents an approach which is attached closely to the philosophy of education. We are not interested in education in so far as education is considered the result of didactically structured arrangements. Instead we are interested in education in so far as it is regarded as an empirically reconstructable process of adoption and assimilation of knowledge (cf. Schuller et al. 2002): where do individuals learn, and which forms of instruction do they opt for? What motives trigger and guide their learning activities? Which knowledge and competences do individuals annex in interaction with their environment, and which concepts of the individual's self and the individual's environment result from these processes of interaction?

Because educational processes are not only based on individual decisions, but also embedded in a socially prestructured realm of possibilities, not only the biographical details recounted on Lifelong Learning, but also the social and historical backgrounds of the various institutional forms of education in which the individuals take part ought to be considered.

The manner in which individuals embrace the manifold forms of education available and the manner in which they thereby constitute themselves as individualized subjects of experience and action, is labeled in our project "Formations of Lifelong Learning" (German: Bildungsgestalten). We consider Formations of Lifelong Learning to be the expression of specific interrelationships between individuality and sociality. Formations of Lifelong Learning are the results of individual decisions concerning educational trajectories, which are embedded in already existent, socially predetermined educational pathways (cf. Pallas 2006).

2.3.1. Time and Formations of Lifelong Learning

Formations of Lifelong Learning outline the profile of an individual's learning biography at a certain point in time. Having two interviews at different points in time therefore allows us to correlate two different imprints of one lifelong educational process. Both formations of Lifelong Learning are considered to be incisions within a chronological process. The project's assumption is that these formations of Lifelong Learning change over the course of time. This change depends not only on the situational and subjective viewpoint of the interviewees, but also on their respective age and the historical backdrop of the interview.

Our research project centers around the different levels at which an impact of time on education becomes apparent.

- The impact of time on education: Level 1 - Biographies
Individuals change over the course of time – they age. This means that they presumably learn new things and they forget how to do other things. It can also be assumed that at different points in the course of their lives, individuals interpret actions they take and events they experience differently. These changes become visible when persons are interviewed over a time span of 25 years. The comparison between the two interviews therefore provides answers to the question of whether and how Formations of Lifelong Learning change over the course of a life.

- The impact of time on education: Level 2 - Generations
Individuals age and so they change their position within the social framework of generations. Probably the individual was 30 years old when the first interview was conducted. The protagonist's main problem might have been the search for a job after a prolonged stage of professional training; he might also have struggled with the question of whether to have children or look for a full-time job. 25 years later many decisions have been taken. The protagonist has managed to raise a family and establish a satisfactory work history. Yet the prospect of retirement appears to be troublesome. With no work and children no longer at home, what is one supposed to do? In this situation, the protagonist might turn towards adult education – probably to pick up hobbies that were abandoned due to a dissociation from his or her own parents (like playing a musical instrument) or, as a consequence of others' encouragement, to learn something new (like how to use a computer). The question of how generation has an impact on formations of Lifelong Learning and how young adults' learning processes differ from those of the aged also plays a role in our project.

- The impact of time on education: Level 3 - History
Our database not only contains biographical information about instruction and learning, it also includes information about the socio-historic context of the observed biographies of instruction and learning. In the interviews conducted in the 1980s, the rise of new social movements (the ecology and peace movement, the women's rights movement) and the

quest to develop new educational settings emerge. The recent interviews have a stronger focus on professional advancement and self-fulfilment.

2.3.2. Change in Formations of Lifelong Learning

The main research focus of our project centers around the continuities and transformations that characterize Formations of Lifelong Learning.

As already mentioned, we postulate an interrelationship between the individual and his social environment when it comes to the realization of education. From that point of view, educational processes are based upon individual decisions which are taken against the backdrop of social contexts, institutional possibilities and individual resources. Since not only the course of an individual's life, but also its social framework is subject to change, we assume that educational processes also change over the course of time.

In contrast to common research on the learning biographies of adults, we take into account the impact of distinct points of time on the unfolding of individual biographies. Our project does not attempt to reconstruct a singular "identity" that emerges out of the two narratives. Instead we aim to elucidate the change that takes place between the Formation of Lifelong Learning I in 1984, and Formation of Lifelong Learning II as we can access it in 2008. Both formations of Lifelong Learning are snapshots in one lifelong educational process. They represent one educational process that spans 25 years and two interviews.

2.4. Formations of Lifelong Learning: Continuity and Transformation

What continuities and transformations within the individual's biography can be found by comparing two interviews that mark a time span of 25 years? Does the individual's age, positioning in the generations framework and place in history make a difference? How does the individual's interpretation of self and environment change? And what role does education play in all of this? Though we cannot give a complete answer to these questions, we want to provide a short insight into the first findings of the project using the example of a female interviewee, whom we will simply call TN41.[3]

---

3 As a means of anonymization all of our interviews carry distinct numbers. These numbers result from the order in which the interviews were conducted in 1984. The two letters provide information on whether the person was interviewed as an attendee (TN) or an instructor (KL).

2.4.1. "I've been a displaced person before I was born": a life history between Continuation and Severance

When the first interview was conducted, TN41 was 40 years old. She was divorced and had no children. She mentioned having grown up in Eastern Germany, but due to severe tension within the family she no longer had any contact with them. She did not mention any other pre-adulthood biographical events. Her biography so far had focused on professional advancement. TN41 had left home soon after finishing school. Then she had started a career as a civil servant. Prior to the first interview, the last four years' work history of her former husband had resulted in three relocations throughout Germany. When another relocation to Berlin caused a dispute, TN41 filed for divorce and moved on her own to an urban region in southern Germany. There she found a well-paid job with a public authority. Regarding TN41's narrative from 1984 it becomes clear that in a time of economic stability she focused primarily on security when it came to the course of her life. Her secure and well paid job was the center of her everyday life, yet she felt dissatisfied with what she was doing. Work always seemed to be done in half the time available. So TN41 sought to compensate by attending adult education classes. She has done this in her free time ever since she was 24. TN41's social life and circle of friends are closely tied to the courses she attends. She has befriended several of her course-mates, most of whom are of the same age. Some friendships have held until 2008. A culturally interested woman of 74 is the only elderly person she has contact with, although their relationship has become quite close. She talks about her instructors as role-models and especially looks up to an instructor on silversmithing who has abandoned his former job to concentrate completely on this.

In 2008 TN41 has followed the silversmith's example. She has taken over the tasks of a drug-consultant and women's representative, concentrating on these tasks to a 100% exclusion of her normal working tasks. For both positions she has voluntarily completed several training courses. She has also founded a women's representative circle spanning several authorities and companies. She finds all these activities fulfilling. Though her activities have resulted in serious conflicts with her work-mates, superiors and even the workers' council, she does not regret them. Her drive to care for others also dominates her life after retirement. She and her new husband have developed large-scale activities to help the children of immigrants through school and professional training. They not only take part in the children's education but also support their parents in legal matters and maintain contact with an extensive network of experts on educational issues, whom they consult when problems arise. Entangled with her account of her commitment to the immigrants' children, biographical accounts of TN41's own childhood emerge. She was a refugee herself. Her father died before she was born. In the course of the Second World War, her mother was forced to flee to Berlin, where TN41 was born in 1943. Having married again, her mother gave birth to six more children, but suffered increasingly from depression. Subsequently TN41 managed to bring up her half-siblings all on her own. TN41 compares the hardships she experienced in the refugee camps with the hardships the immigrants' children experience today. The refugees from the former eastern regions of the collapsing "Third Reich" were despised by the inhabitants of Berlin, just like immigrants are disliked by some Germans nowadays. In her narratives, the picture she paints of her mother closely resembles the portrayal of the immigrant mothers. Yet TN41 does not see her current commitment to disadvantaged children as a continuation of her childhood tasks. Today, as she puts it, she is doing something totally different. Considering the memories of her mother, she has never wanted to have children herself. On the other hand the immigrants' children and to a lesser extent their parents have become a replacement family for TN41. Whereas she still has little contact with her original family, she enjoys the company of the children she cares for. When TN41 returned from a serious operation due to pancreatic cancer, the children and their families arranged an impressive celebration to welcome her back home. This, TN41 states, is something you would not expect your own children to do.

3. Conclusion

The project's first findings point out that the attempt to compare different Formations of Lifelong Learning experienced by one and the same person at two different times in the course of their life yields new insights into the instruction and learning of adults.

Of course we find within our sample archetypal formations of "identities". The individual's own development is depicted as the constant unfolding of a personal nucleus that seems to be existent from the very start of the person's life. Such Formations of Lifelong Learning are more or less on par with the traditional ideal of education and "Bildung" as a means of personal perfection. Other interviews, like the previously mentioned case of TN41 as well as the majority of our cases, demonstrate that the traditional ideal of personal perfection ("Bildung") might probably not be the prevailing type of learning in a person's life. Given the example of TN41, it is not the unfolding of an already existing identity that leads to the variety of learning and instructional activities as well as the social commitment which our protagonist develops. Instead it is the permanent tension between biographical continuities and transformations that the individual is confronted with that finally leads to the specific Formation of Lifelong Learning we can observe in this case. Over the course of her life TN41 has been confronted with a wide variety of events and impressions. Some she tries to embrace (like the personal satisfaction she experiences on courses in silversmithing), whilst others she tries to forget (like her childhood years as a refugee). At certain points in her life things that have been conserved so far are scrutinized and subject to abandonment (like her focus on vocational advancement), whereas other topics that have been repressed become important again and trigger new learning activities (like her care for people in need).

The "identity" of TN41 is thus not static but fluid, changing over the course of time. Considering other cases in the project one can reason that it is not so much a static identity – and with that a continuously advancing learning biography – that guarantees personal happiness, but rather a flexible, changeable formation of identity which can be individually attuned over and over again to the current realities. This seems reasonable, since individuals – as living beings – change. They age, they take over different positions in the generations framework and they are subject to historical change.

In the future, biographical research on adult education should take a closer look at the interrelationship between time and educational processes and at the impact of time on biographies and Formations of Lifelong Learning. The individual's position in biographical, generational and historical time has to be taken into account more than has been the case until now. It is not sufficient merely to correlate age and learning activities, as several Adult Education Surveys do; individuals' perceptions and interpretations of themselves in time as well as of the educational processes that take place in that time must also be considered. Our research project indicates that qualitative studies on this are a necessary addition to quantitative surveys on adult learning.

References

Alheit, P. (2009): Diskursive Politiken – Lebenslanges Lernen als Surrogat? In: Hof, Ch./Ludwig, J./Zeuner, Ch. (ed.): Strukturen Lebenslangen Lernens. Baltmannsweiler, p. 4-14.

Alheit, P./Dausien, B. (2002): Bildungsprozesse über die Lebensspanne und lebenslanges Lernen. In: Tippelt, R. (ed.): Handbuch Bildungsforschung. Opladen, p. 565-585.

Beck, U./Beck-Gernsheim, E. (1994) (ed.): Riskante Freiheiten. Frankfurt/Main.

Beck, U./Bonß, W. (2001) (ed.): Die Modernisierung der Moderne. Frankfurt/Main.

Beck, U./Giddens, A./Lash, S. (1996): Reflexive Modernisierung. Eine Kontroverse. Frankfurt/Main.

Beck, U./Lau, C. (2004) (ed.): Entgrenzung und Entscheidung. Frankfurt/Main.

Bolder, A./Hendrich, W. (2000): Fremde Bildungswelten. Alternative Strategien lebenslangen Lernens. Opladen.

Brödel, R. (2009): Lebenslanges Lernen. In: Hof, C./Fuhr, T./Gonon, P. (ed.): Handbuch der Erwachsenenbildung/Weiterbildung. Paderborn, p. 975-986.

Coffield, F. (1999): Breaking the Consensus: Lifelong Learning as social control. In: British Educational Research Journal, 25 (4), p. 479-499.

Fischer-Rosenthal, W. (2005): The Problem with Identity: Biography as Solution to Some (Post)-Modernist Dilemmas. In: Comenius 15 /1995. Reprint in: Miller, R. L. (2005) (ed.) Biographical Research Methods. Volume 2, p. 213-230.

Fischer, M. E. (2007): Raum und Zeit: Das Lernen Erwachsener aus Sicht der Modernisierungstheorie. Hohengehren.

Forneck, J. (2001): Die große Aspiration: Lebenslanges, selbstgesteuertes Lernen. In: EB - Vierteljahresschrift für Theorie & Praxis 47 (4), p. 158-163.

Giddens, A. (1984): The constitution of society. Berkeley.

Giddens, A. (1990): The consequences of modernity. Stanford.

Herzberg, H. (2004): Biographie und Lernhabitus. Eine Studie im Rostocker Werftarbeitermilieu. Frankfurt/Main.

Hof, C. (2009): Lebenslanges Lernen. Eine Einführung. Stuttgart

Hof, C./Kade, J. (2009): Prekäre Kontinuitäten. Das lebenslange Lernen aus biographietheoretischer Perspektive im Rahmen einer Follow-up-Studie. In: Hof, C./Ludwig, J./Zeuner, C. (ed.): Strukturen Lebenslangen Lernens. Hohengehren, p. 150-160.

Kade, J. (1989): Erwachsenenbildung und Identität. Weinheim.

Kade, J. (1991): Diffuse Zielgerichtetheit. Rekonstruktion einer unabgeschlossenen Bildungsbiographie. In: Tietgens, H. (ed.): Kommunikation in Lehr-Lern-Prozessen mit Erwachsenen, p. 94-111.

Kade, J. (1997): Riskante Biographien und die Risiken des lebenslangen Lernens. In: Report. Literatur- und Forschungsreport Weiterbildung 39, p. 112-124.

Kade, J./Hof, C. (2007): Biographie und Lebenslauf. Über ein biographietheoretisches Projekt zum lebenslangen Lernen auf der Grundlage wiederholter Erhebungen. In: Felden, H. v. (ed.): Perspektiven erziehungswissenschaftlicher Biographieforschung. Wiesbaden, p.159-176.

Kade, J./Hof, C. (2009): Die Zeit der (erziehungswissenschaftlichen) Biographieforschung. In: Ecarius, J./Schäffer, B.(ed.): Typenbildung und Theoriegenerierung. Methoden und Methodologien qualitativer Biographie- und Bildungsforschung. Opladen.

Kade, J./Hof, C./Peterhoff, D. (2008): Verzeitlichte Bildungsgestalten: Subjektbildung im Kontext des Lebenslangen Lernens. In: Report. Forschungsreport Weiterbildung. Issue 4/2008.

Kade, J./Seitter, W. (1996): Lebenslanges Lernen. Mögliche Bildungswelten. Opladen.

Kade, J./Seitter, W. (1998): Bildung - Risiko - Genuß. Dimensionen und Ambivalenzen lebenslangen Lernens. In: Brödel, R. (ed.) (1998): Lebenslanges Lernen - lebensbegleitende Bildung, p. 51-59.

Kade, J./Seitter, W. (2003): Jenseits des Goldstandards. In: Helsper, W./Hörster, R./Kade, J. (ed.) (2003): Ungewissheit. Pädagogische Felder im Modernisierungsprozess, p. 50-72.

Kade, J./Seitter, W. (2007): Lebenslanges Lernen. In: Göhlich, M./Wulf, Chr./Zirfas, J. (ed.): Pädagogische Theorien des Lernens. Weinheim, p. 133-141.

EU Commission of the European Communities (2000): Memorandum on Lifelong Learning. Brussels.

Nohl, A.-M. (2006b): Interview und dokumentarische Methode. Anleitungen für die Forschungspraxis. Wiesbaden.

Pallas, A.M. (2006): Educational Transitions, Trajectories and Pathways. In: Mortimer, J.T.; Shanahan, M.J. (ed.) (2006): Handbook of the Life Course. Series: Handbooks of Sociology and Social Research. New York, p. 165-184.

Schuller, T., Brassett-Grundy, A., Green, A., Hammond, C. and Preston, J. (2002): Learning, Continuity and Change in Adult Life, Wider Benefits of Learning Research Report No. 3. Centre for Research on the Wider Benefits of Learning, London: Institute of Education.

Strauss, A./Corbin J. (1996): Grounded Theory. Grundlagen Qualitativer Sozialforschung. Weinheim.

Desire as Response to Experience: On Motivational Aspects of Learning

Ulla Thøgersen

Introduction

When the researcher of adult learning asks the question "how does the adult individual learn in and through work?" she finds no theoretical consensus in the research field regarding what learning is. Different theoretical platforms can be distinguished depending on their ontological perspective on learning: is learning a phenomenon existing in individual, interpersonal or contextual compositions, e.g. should we locate learning in cognitive processes, communication or organisational structures? From a pragmatic standpoint it seems that all these perspectives hold some part of the truth as human existence is a complex matter and in turning to only one perspective we risk overlooking this complexity. It can be argued that learning is linked to the individual – someone is learning something – but also that learning is intimately linked to the social context in which the individual acts since human existence is always already a life with others. This opening statement tells us that a key factor in learning theory is to discuss our understanding of human existence. Any theoretical description of learning will be based on assumptions about human existence whether or not the theory explicitly argues for these assumptions.

The perspective in this paper is that learning is a human condition: we cannot escape to learn something in our lives and through learning we build up habits as patterns of meaning which function as relatively stable rhythms in life. The rhythms are only relatively stable as they can be contested by new learning processes or due to other reasons for changes in our capacity. This also means that learning takes place in different forms or settings. In this sense this paper is in agreement with Jarvis, who writes: *"learning is wider than education: education is only one social institution in which learning occurs, albeit the only one specifically di-*

rected toward it. (...) But all the social institutions together cannot contain learning, since learning is fundamental to human being and to life itself." (Jarvis 1992:10). This perspective rebels against the patent of the educational system to claim "learning" as its territory and it opens up the perspective that learning occurs in all spheres of life, including working life. In relation to the workplace setting learning processes can be found as an integrated (and unplanned as such) part of the daily work as well as it can take place within planned learning situations directed explicitly at learning (see Antonacopoulou et al. 2005; Billett et al. 2006).

These reflections do not mean that learning just happens by itself, but learning is the result of an activity situated in the context of an individual existence. Hence, learning is related to the way the individual takes up a position within the world and the direction and meaning integrated in this position. Learning can take place in different settings – work, education, leisure time – but it is always linked to the action of an individual learner. Hence, a central aspect to consider when researching or facilitating learning in any setting is the learner's motivation to engage in learning processes: What is the instigator of learning? Or formulated differently: How does the learning process start up and stay in motion? What is at stake in our actions which brings us to learning? It has been described that learning can be incidental in the sense that it is a by-product of some activity in which learning is not meant or intended to happen (Marsick and Watkins 1990); but I would argue that it is unlikely that learning as such can be radically separated from the motivations (or meanings) which start up an action. The idea of incidental learning forms a dichotomy between non-intentional and intentional learning which does not take into account the complexity of human action (see also Garrick 1998). Phenomenological philosophy has contested the idea that the concept of intention should be the starting point for inquiry into human action; instead phenomenology suggests the concept of intentionality which means that human action is always directed at something, but the direction does not have to be either based on clear intentions behind the actions or be an incidental (non-intended) product of an intended activity (see Husserl 2001; Merleau-Ponty 1962; Pietersma 2000; Sokolowski 2000). Our intentionality, our direction in the world, is bound to an open-ended process of meaning anchored in the dynamic interrelation of the individual and the lived (social) world. From this perspective the real challenge in relation to motivation is to understand how the different spheres of meaning work together in human life and through this understanding provide an answer to how the learning activity starts up and stays in motion.

Existing theoretical conceptualizations of motivation provide us with a range of understandings which carry different practical implications in relation to the possibilities of organizing planned learning situations based on participant motivation (e.g. Maslow 1954, McClelland 1961, McGregor 1960). This paper is aimed at discussing motivation in relation to adult learning by taking seriously the question: How does the learning process start up and stay in motion? The paper consists of two "moves" in relation to this question.

1) In the first move the paper critically discusses the answers given by classic need gratification theory (Maslow 1954, McClelland 1961, McGregor 1960) and by learning theories placed within the field of workplace learning or organizational learning (Senge 1990, Argyris et Schön 1978, 1996, Wenger 1998) and it opens up the ambition to rethink motivation from the point of view of a phenomenological understanding of desire.

2) The second move follows up on this ambition by presenting an understanding of desire within a phenomenological framework (Merleau-Ponty 1962) and by discussing the implication of a shift in focus from needs to desire in relation to planning learning situations based on participant motivation.

Motivation, work and learning: critical perspectives

Theories of motivation often pinpoint motivation in relation to certain subjective "motives": needs, drives, instincts, expectations and goals. I do something *because* I am trying to realize a goal or because I have a need I want to satisfy. Vroom and Deci writes: *"most conceptions of the process of motivation begin with the assumption that behavior is, at least in part, directed towards the attainment of goals or towards the satisfaction of needs or motives"* (Vroom et Deci 1970:21). A recent publication titled *The Passion of Organizing* agrees with this (Brewis et al. 2007). At the same time the authors suggest that the particular question "why do we work" is primarily answered in the context of need gratification theory. In relation to work motivation and business management they write: *"The classic motivation theories (and Maslow and Herzberg in particular) are still taught routinely – and globally – as part of business studies curricula, to all levels of students. What is more, they have come to form a fairly stable bedrock for a great deal of management activity (...) The influence of Maslow's sixty year old theory is visible in a wide range of contemporary management techniques and approaches, including TQM, BPR, empowerment and self-management teams."* (Brewis et al. 2007). The quote refers to a classic framework for understanding motivation especially linked to the concept of need (e.g. Maslow 1954, McClelland 1961). In this framework motivation is structured as an overall drive stemming from some form of lack related to the subject which pushes the subject towards an end situation in which the lack is overcome and disappears. In relation to learning specifically, motivation can be presumed to be present, *only if* the content of the learning process is experienced as being a means or an end to satisfying the particular need. Maslow and McClelland famously point to different forms of particular needs, e.g. physiological needs, needs for safety, love needs, esteem needs and self-actualization needs (Maslow 1954) and needs for achievement, power and affiliation (McClelland 1961) which in turn is used to explain why we work and also secondarily why we learn at work. Both also share the common assumption that motivation is linked to an understanding of a human being as a *"wanting animal"* (Maslow 1954:7). This assumption is also shared by McGregor in relation to his description of theory X and theory Y in *The Human side of enterprise*: *"Man is a wanting animal – as soon as one of his needs is satisfied another appears in its place. This process is unending. It continues from birth to death. Man continuously puts forth effort – works, if you please – to satisfy his needs."* (McGregor 1960:36).

The need theories of motivation are primarily focused on motivation as stemming from "inside" the subject as an internal drive behind our action. Maslow writes about learning: *"... the theory of basic needs presented here is a theory of ends and ultimate values of the organism. These ends are intrinsically, and in themselves, valuable to the organism. It will do anything necessary to achieve these goals, even to learning arbitrary, irrelevant, trivial or silly procedures that an experimenter may set up as the only way to get to these goals."* (Maslow 1954:35). Maslow's theoretical framework is focused on the stated ends connected to the intrinsic values of the subject. When the theory is employed in relation to organizing planned learning situations emphasis is primarily put on the subject. The perspective on needs essentially locates the ground of motivation outside the learning environment since needs operate as a drive behind our actions. Hence the learning situation can be seen as the means to satisfying already existing needs and will be viewed in terms of its suitability, e.g. the situation can place obstacles in the way of reaching satisfaction or attaining a goal.

More recent theories on adult learning in the work context provide answers to the question "why do we learn (at work)" which in part depart from need gratification theory. Within the field of organizational learning Peter Senge tells us that learning organizations are possible because learning not only is an integral part of human nature, but also because we have a fundamental love for learning (Senge 1990). If we accept Senge's standpoint we should be able to presume that the motivation to learn is at any time present. However, most learning theories are less radical and assume that motivation is not to be understood as a fundamental readiness-to-learn anything at any given time.

Argyris and Schön provide a different understanding of motivation related to their ideas on learning as correction of mismatch between expectations and actions (Argyris et Schön 1978, 1996). In this framework motivation can be said to be grounded in a general "existential" purpose of sustaining a balance (match) between expectations and actions; the motivation to learn is instigated as "a need" to reestablish this balance if it is disturbed – or in other words: to return to stable conditions. This view can primarily be used to understand the motivation to learn in relation to an already existing problem, but is more difficult to employ if the focus is to organize planned learning situations; at least in the sense that if the problem (mismatch) is not already present for the learner, the learning situation has only the option of initiating participant motivation *by* creating a mismatch somehow, namely to create an unbalance, an unstable condition which can prompt the learning process. Otherwise planned learning activities are mainly presented as interventions in relation to mismatch situations.

In his social theory of learning presented in *Communities of Practice* Wenger identifies a different ground of motivation when he speaks of the learning process as negotiation of meaning based on reification and participation (Wenger 1998). His definition of meaning can be seen as an attempt to find a motivational essence of learning, namely the participant engagement at stake in learning processes. He points to meaning negotiation as a key in learning and defines meaning as *"our ability to experience the world and our engagement in it as meaningful."* (Wenger 1998:4). This definition can be criticized for being somewhat circular: meaning is what is meaningful. Hence it can be argued that Wenger identifies meaning as the starting place for the learning process, however without really clarifying the nature of meaning. Hence this view on motivation is also difficult to employ in planning learning situations in the sense that "where do we start": how do we create meaning through an experience of the meaningful?

The concept of meaning seems central to understanding motivation. The concept opens our eyes to the plurality of concrete meanings that individuals can experience. It can be made into a point and not a criticism that the experience of meaning can be generalized in relation to human beings as such, but the concrete experience of meaning can only be fully named in relation to the individual: what I find meaningful might not be what you find meaningful. The experience of meaning can hence incorporate different interests linked to the individual being. However, the weakness is that the concept of meaning alone might cause us to lose sight of phenomena which motivate us generally *as* humans, namely the relation of what is meaningful to certain (motivating) phenomena, for instance needs, expectations or desires. In other words: it might be useful to provide a link between a concept of meaning and theoretical reflections on motivation. If the purpose is to create a learning environment then this link can be useful in determining general factors in creating meaningful experiences for the participants which in turn can motivate the learning process.

The publication *The Passion of Organizing* provides an interesting alternative to the theoretical perspectives of motivation as listed above (Brewis et al. 2007). The authors write from within critical management studies and their common "mission" is to rethink motivation theory. The main move of their argument is to depart from need gratification theory and "*excavate other systems of representation*" which will provide alternative answers to "why do we work?" (Brewis et al. 2007:19). They criticize need gratification theory for its view of the human being as deficient and argue that this view on the one hand does not match reality (life as we live it); and on the other hand does not take account of philosophical inquiries into alternative views, e.g. views on passionate experience (see Silverman 2000). The authors are concerned with widening the focus on motivation to incorporate elements which otherwise fall outside the model of the human being as a wanting animal. Their alternative answer is built around three elements:

1. Attentiveness to the "dark sides" of motivation, namely the possibility of obsession, addiction, violence.

2. An alternative description of desire as something other than desire-as-lack, namely as a creative force that produces motivation.
3. Reflections on the complexities of work experience beyond instrumentality, including joy, laughter, anxiety, friendship and hate.

In particular interest is here the second element: the alternative description of desire. The second part of *The Passion of Organizing* is titled "Motivation and desire". The authors are interested in presenting perspectives on desire which depart from the idea of desire-as-lack and instead bring attention to desire as a creative force that produces motivation. This interest coincides with this paper which is also aimed at contributing to reflections on desire in order to bring forth an alternative understanding of motivation in relation to need gratification theory. Based on phenomenological philosophy desire can be said to form an important ground of motivation. However, desire is not to be understood as an internal lack in the subject, but as response to experience. This reflection contrasts desire with need in the sense that desire operates as a pull from the experienced world and thus works "in between" our actions as ways of relating to the experienced world. A focus on desire also places a different obligation with the organizer planning a learning situation than the concept of need since desire is located as a response to experience in the interplay of embodied subject and environment. Hence the learning situation should be actively created as a 'desirable' environment which inspires the learner; rather than motivation is to be "discovered" as originating from outside the situation leaving the organizer with the job of matching need and learning situation the best possible way in order to engage the participants.

With this aim the paper is in accordance with the main argument of *The Passion of Organizing*: to rethink motivation theory by widening its focus to include desire as passionate being; however it also departs from its specific arguments on desire in two central ways:

Firstly, *The Passion of Organizing* is primarily focused on the philosophical descriptions of desire in Deleuze and Guattari (e.g. Styhre 2007). This paper, however, has a different starting point since it finds its arguments within phenomenological philosophy of Merleau-Ponty (1962/1945). The phenomenology of Merleau-Ponty allows us to bring in reflections on embodiment and pay attention to the lived experience of desire.

Secondly, the paper places the reflections on motivation in relation to learning. *The Passion of Organizing* is focused mainly on work motivation. This paper, however, is concerned with bringing ideas on desire and motivation in relation to learning and to discuss the implications of theoretical perspectives of motivation in relation to planning learning situations.

The following part of the paper is divided into two sections. The first section investigates the understanding of desire as response to experience. The second section discusses this understanding in relation to adult learning.

Desire as response to experience

The phenomenology of Merleau-Ponty enables us to approach desire in a different way than an understanding of desire-as-lack. Merleau-Ponty points us to an original embodied rhythm in human existence in which experience is not based solely on subjective intentions, but primarily on my attention and response to the things experienced (Merleau-Ponty 1962; Waldenfels 2000). Merleau-Ponty underlines that experience is intrinsically an expressive event, namely an event bringing meaning to the world. In experience I take up a particular position in the experienced world because of a continual attention to the world around me and because the body agrees to follow the demand of the things experienced to be realized as meaning. In this sense experience is responsive – and the recurrent movement between experience and expression forms an original rhythm of life in which we are engaged as embodied beings. In this movement we do not represent an experience in expression by meeting the thing experienced with clear intentions, but Merleau-Ponty says that there is an "emotional essence" within the intertwining of experience, expression and meaning which calls us in experience and demands an expression in the first place (Merleau-Ponty 1962:182ff).

From this perspective on human existence it can be argued that desire is not based on lack, but on the experience of emotional meaning or more specifically: desire originates as a response to an affective experience of attractive otherness[4]; an experience in which the otherness takes

---

4 The term "otherness" is used to indicate that desire is directed at something other than the subject of desire itself; this however does not limit desire to being

form as 'the desired' (Merleau-Ponty 1962: 154ff). Hence the desired is not desired because it can satisfy a desire already present as a fundamental need in the subject, but the desired is part of the origin of desire. Desire begins in otherness. In my experience *something* in the world evokes my desire because this 'something' attracts me. My bodily existence is troubled through the way something in the world addresses my bodily being. Hence the intentionality of desire is to be distinguished from needs as well as from intellectual will. Desire is neither an a priori given state of need in the organism nor is desire produced by an act of will. I cannot produce desire by willing that "I desire X", but desire erupts spontaneously in my experience of otherness. Hence there is an element of passivity in desire. It can be compared to the difference between the calm sea and the troubled sea. Something has troubled the sea and this "something" is beyond the control of the sea itself. There is an element of passivity in the transition from the calm sea to the troubled sea. The same is true of desire. My whole existence has been shaken through the way the otherness addresses my bodily being. This description also corresponds to popular expressions of desire (erotic desire mainly) in fiction: desire as an earthquake, a river run wild, a lightning strike or a volcano. These metaphors all have in common that they represent something beyond our control (Belsey 1994). I am *being affected*. Desire is enclosed in the experience itself as something *that happens*; however it is not a matter of causal stimulus from the environment as I do not necessarily respond to the same phenomena the same way over and over again, but the emotional meanings can change in the temporality of the individual.

Need gratification theory places the origin of motivation outside the experience of the world as something which is internally connected to the state of the subject while Merleau-Ponty places the origin of desire within experience. Desire is initiated through experience. The experience forms a mode of subjectivity which transforms my situation: I become a desiring subject. In this sense desire is not produced by the subject, but *entered*. The desiring mode of subjectivity is characterised by a

---

directed at "the other" understood as another person, but desire is broadly understood as an emotional field in human existence defined by a passionate striving to attach the desiring subject to particular elements (something) in the world, namely the desired object.

call to unfold the experience of desire. Desire demands that I devote myself to it by taking it up and living it. It is not enough for desire to exist as a troubled body, but desire is always beyond itself in the sense that it seeks to relate itself to the desired. In other words: desire takes is placed in the midst of the lived experience as the tending of the body towards the desired other. Desire can be said to motivate my actions because desire opens up a preference or a dimension of value to my existence. When I enter the experience of desire I am directed towards the desired (the desired attracts me) and my existence is opened up as a form of communication with the desired in the sense that desire transcends the subject and brings me to the desired. Desmond writes in accordance with Merleau-Ponty: *"Desire erupts in experience; it does so spontaneously and, to that extent, is immediate. But beyond its initial, spontaneous upsurge, it may unfold in an articulated, mediated way."* (Desmond 1987:9). In desire there is not one given a priori response. The answer to the expression of desire does not lie in the logic of desire itself. What we have encountered is that desire motivates, but at the same time desire can go anywhere depending on for instance the cultural context surrounding the desiring subject and the individual experiences of past desires, e.g. the experience of successful or disappointed desires.

From this perspective desire can be understood as an emotional field in human existence defined by both a passionate striving to attach oneself to the world or more specifically particular elements in the world (the desired object) *and* a dynamic intense movement directed at realizing this attachment as a particular communication with the desired object. Desire in this broad sense expresses a horizon of meaning from which life takes a direction. It comes forth as concrete passions defined by a particular time and space since its origin is related to the experience of the desired object, but also spreads out as an emotional background or atmosphere underlying our actions more generally by setting an emotional tone of our experience of the world.

This account of desire implies a shift of focus which is important in relation to motivation theory. The focus is changed from the internal drives of the subject to the interplay in experience between the embodied person and the perceived world. This shift holds part of the criticism of needs gratification theory as the basis of understanding motivation and it points to motivation as linked to an emotional engagement into the lived world. It departs from a theory-of-lack or an idea of human being as a wanting animal. Instead the concept of desire points to an experience of engagement based on what we could call 'a surplus' in experience in the sense that something in desire takes on a meaning for me which changes my mode of subjectivity in terms of an emotional engagement.

The shift in focus from internal drives to engagement means that it is also urgent to discuss the concept of motivation itself: how well suited is the concept of motivation to identify the engaged movements of the subject in the world? The concept of motivation implies some form of "motive" behind the action related to the subject. However, the phenomenological concept of desire surpasses a distinction between inner and outer, between experience and action. Desire is *not* a drama happening in an inner state of consciousness, which then – as its next step – needs to find itself a public version. On the contrary: desire takes place in the world as an engagement with the world. Hence from this perspective it makes sense to talk of engagement rather than motivation since desire is to be engaged in a situation rather than to carry an internal motive to the situation. The authors of *The Passion of organizing* open a similar discussion when they write: *"...we might argue that the idea of motivation itself is somewhat stultifying; that it is discursively imbued through and through with the assumptions of content, process and reinforcement theory, such that its invocation makes it difficult to think beyond the idea that individuals are motivated by some form of internal need-deficiency or external stimulus (whether enjoyable or unpleasant) or that their motivation rests on a rational calculation of the outcomes of the behavior."* (Brewis et al. 2007). In other word: there is a risk that the concept of motivation brings us to focus on the subject by its inherent idea of motives and as such makes it difficult to rethink motivation in terms of experience and meaning embedded in the intertwining of subject and world.

Desire and learning

A particular interest in this paper is to discuss motivation theory in relation to learning. It has been presented that within the context of need gratification theory the motivation for learning is present, only insofar the learning process is a means to an end to satisfying a particular need (Maslow 1954, McClelland 1961, McGregor 1960). This is a very limited way of understanding motivation which excludes that motivation can be brought about by providing inspiring learning environments. The perspective on needs locates the ground of motivation outside the learning environment and the learning situation has to be organized in relation to its suitability of satisfying already existing subjective needs. A similar situation goes for Argyris and Schön: the motivation to learn is found in an already existing problem situation (a mismatch/missing balance) and is thus an expression of another sort of 'need': the need to sustain a match/balance within the relation of subject and world (Argyris et Schön 1978, 1996). If the problem situation is not present, the motivation to learn is not instigated. Hence, the learning situation has to be planned either as interventions to an existing mismatch or it has to bring forth some form of mismatch in order for the participant to be engaged in learning.

The phenomenological focus on desire places a different obligation with the learning situation since desire is located as a response to experience in the interplay of embodied subject and environment. Hence it is possible to create "desirable" learning situations which inspire the learner and open up the experience of desire. Initiatives can be carried through with the purpose of engaging the student. This understanding is more in line with Wenger in the sense that his theory underlines meaning as "the motivational essence" of learning (Wenger 1998). Despite his circular definition of meaning, he points to something important: meaning is not enclosed in the perspective of the individual, but meaning is experienced within a constant negotiation process in which the relation to otherness (the world as such, other people) is central (Wenger 1998). A similar point is made by Merleau-Ponty: meaning is linked to experience in which I take up a position in the world because of an attention to the world around me and because the body agrees to follow the demand of the experienced world to be realized as meaning. In this sense experience (meaning) is responsive, but not determined (Merleau-Ponty 1962). Meaning can be viewed as communication within an intimate bond between the individual and the world. In relation to motivation, it is of importance that Merleau-Ponty links the process of meaning to an "emotional essence" which calls us into experience. Hence, the philosophy of Merleau-Ponty allows us to break with the idea that learning is motivated by clear intentions or clear-cut goals which are determined prior to the engagement into the learning situations. The concept of desire tells us how the motivation to learn is a response to the learning situation. In the learning situation desire can be born through an inspired experience. To conclude this paper two central points are to be made:

Firstly, this paper has argued that desire can be "sparked" through the organization of the learning situation. Hence, it is possible to "seduce" – so to speak – the possible learners to learn something in particular. The seduction sets the learner in motion. It engages the participant to transcend him- or herself in a movement toward the desired. In other words desire opens up the possibilities of learning, of bringing the perspectives of otherness in play. If the subject is placed in an immanent context of self-reference nothing new can come to the subject, nothing can in principle be learned, but the subject is forced to repeat the same meanings. In a phenomenological perspective absolute immanence is impossible since a human being is characterized by openness to the world: we are always transcending ourselves. In planning a learning situation it can be attempted to direct the process of transcendence by engaging the learner in an inspired experience of desire. This in turn emphasizes the importance of pedagogy or didactics – since the motivation to learn is intimately linked to the didactic approaches of the organizer.

Secondly, it must be stated that the direction of desire cannot be fully planned, on the contrary: when desire is experienced the individual expresses his or her desire by taking it up and living it – not within an a priori determined logic of desire, but as a living phenomenon which can in principle go anywhere. This also means that desire can have a "darker" side: it might not be unproblematic to seduce/inspire someone, but the learner can become fixated, obsessed and violent as an expression of desire. This point also opens up questions of morality. So far nothing normative has been said about the "seduction" linked to desire, but a few notes must be made. In principle learning is not normative in the sense that learning in itself cannot explain if the learning is good or bad. However, in planning learning situations, the organizer is attempting to foster learning processes by directing the learners' desire towards particular learning processes. The organizer must acknowledge a moral responsibility. There is an obligation with the organizer to consider how the desires can both support and/or interfere with the purposes of learning, and the organizer must look at the consequences concerning the way she/he organizes the learning situations in relation to the experiences of desire. A main point to be taken from this paper is that learning does not take place in a neutral world stripped of all desires, but what we learn, how we learn is related to desires (or missing desires) connected to the learning situation – and our desires in turn are continuously initiated and shaped by the learning situation.

References

Antonacopoulou E., Jarvis P., Andersen V., Elkjaer B. & Høyrup, S. (eds.) 2005. Learning, Working and Living. Mapping the Terrain of Working Life Learning, New York: Palgrave Macmillan

Argyris, C. & Schön, D.A. 1978. Organizational Learning. A Theory of Action Perspective, New York: Addison-Wesley

Argyris, C. and Schön, D.A. 1996. Organizational Learning 2: Theory, Method and Practice, New York: Addison-Wesley

Belsey, C. 1994. Desire. Love stories in Western Culture, Oxford: Blackwell Publishers

Billett, S., Fenwick, T. & Somerville, M. (eds.) 2006. Work, Subjectivity and Learning. Understanding learning through Working Life, Dordrecht: Springer

Brewis, J., Linstead, S., Boje, D. & O'Shea, T. (eds.) 2007. The Passion of Organizing, Copenhagen: Liber and Copenhagen Business School Press

Husserl, E. 2001. Logical Investigations. Volume I-II. London: Routledge.

Jarvis, P. 1992. Paradoxes of Learning. On becoming an individual in society, San Francisco: Jossey-Bass Publishers

Maslow, A.H. 1954. Motivation and Personality, New York: Addison Wesley

McClelland, D.C. 1961. The Achieving Society, Princeton: Van Nostrand

McGregor, D. 1960. The Human side of Enterprise, New York: McGraw-Hill

Merleau-Ponty, M. 1964. Sense and Non-sense, Evanston: Northwestern University Press

Merleau-Ponty, M. 1962. Phenomenology of Perception, London: Routledge & Kegan

Merleau-Ponty, M. 1945. Phénoménologie de la Perception. Paris: Gallimard

Pietersma, H. 2000. Phenomenological Epistemology, Oxford: Oxford University Press.

Senge, P.M. 1990. The Fifth Discipline. The Art and Practice of the Learning Organization, New York: Currency Double Day

Sokolowski, R. 2000. Introduction to Phenomenology, Cambridge: Cambridge University Press

Silverman, H.J. (ed.) 2000. Philosophy and desire. New York: Routledge

Styhre, A. Deleuze, Desire and Motivation Theory. In Brewis, J., Linstead, S., Boje, D. & O'Shea, T. (eds.) 2007. The Passion of Organizing, Copenhagen: Liber and Copenhagen Business School Press

Vroom, V.H. & Deci, E.L. (eds.) 1970. Management and Motivation. Selected Readings, New York: Penguin Books

Waldenfels, B. The Paradox of Expression. In Evans, F. & Lawlor L. (eds.) 2000. Chiasms: Merleau-Ponty's notion of flesh. New York: State University of New York Press.

Wenger, E. 1998. Communities of Practice. Learning, Meaning and Identity. Cambridge: Cambridge University Press

Social construction of meaning and its translation into real world action: the problem of learning transfer and how to circumvent it

Søren Willert

The article has three sections followed by concluding remarks. In the first section I present a model naming and showing structural relationships between four media through which human learning may be channelled. The second section discusses the learning transfer problem as it may be conceived through the theoretical logic lying behind this model. In the third section, certain design features of a newly established Master Programme in Organizational Coaching aimed at circumventing the learning transfer problem are described. Concluding remarks draw general implications for University teaching programmes.

1. Four media facilitating human learning

Most parsimoniously described, human learning manifests itself through temporal pattern changes of a relatively stable nature. The learner's potential for or manifest ways of relating himself to himself or to his external environment is affected. Patterns undergoing change as part of a learning process must necessarily be rooted in some medium or other. I shall present a model based on the idea that four pattern-sustaining media are available as possible vehicles for human learning. The model has taxonomic aspirations meaning that, until otherwise convinced, I shall maintain that, at the given level of abstraction, any possible learning instance to be encountered may be accounted for through the model.

The four pattern-sustaining, learning-facilitating media included in the model are the following (in their order of appearance below): languageing, experiential awareness, bodily action, and social exchange structures.

Figure 1 shows how the four media of the model are related along two dimensions. One dimension is named social / individual: Is the medium situated in social space, i.e. implying the structured interplay between a number of actors, or is it monitored by one individual actor all by him- or herself? The other dimension is named mental / behavioural: Is the medium situated in mental space, i.e. dealing with symbolically expressed meaning (ideational contents), or does it involve concretely meaningful activity observable in physical time-space?

Figure 1: Four learning media and their interrelatedness

	Mental	Behavioural
Social	**Languageing**	**Social exchange structure**
Individual	**Experiential awareness**	**Bodily action**

The following sub-sections present a rough sketch of the different forms of learning that may be facilitated through the four media.

Learning forms and media are presented one by one. In natural settings where learning is involved more than one medium will typically be activated. My reasons for isolating the media in the exposition below will become clear when I reach section 2 dealing with the learning transfer problem.

Learning mediated through languageing
Terminology: Languageing is a term used in systemic and social constructionist literature denoting language as a medium for social discourse. Languageing, of course, involves physical activity observable in time-space, but what makes languageing interesting (in the context of this article) is its capacity to bring about meaning coordination (Barnett Pearce, 2007) between actors bringing widely divergent meaning universes to their joint conversation. These are my reasons

for placing the languageing medium in the category of 'mental & social'.

What kind(s) of learning? Languageing goes on all the time as an indispensable ingredient in human living and learning. Achieving languageing-based learning is the stated immediate objective of a wide variety of professional helping dialogues: psychotherapy, counselling, coaching, etc. The client meets the professional helper with a narrative about 'something', i.e. some state of affairs, that is somehow seen as unsatisfactory. In the ensuing helping dialogue, the dialogical partners are in contact with this state of affairs only through linguistic means. Likewise, their efforts to do something about the unsatisfactory state of affairs take the form of joint languageing. The professional person seeks to help his client by facilitating various kinds of changes: expansion, restructuring, correction, clarification, etc., in the way the client talks about the said state of affairs.

The classroom is another setting intended to bring about languageing-based learning. Compared with what is typically the case in the professional helping dialogue, the professional guardian of classroom languageing, i.e. the teacher, will probably play a more decisive role in shaping its form and content (even if more student-centered approaches have also been developed). In spite of such differences (and more could be named), the two kinds of learning encounters are 'two of a kind' in that languageing is their preferred medium for learning facilitation. Through rote learning, through teachers' talk, through discussions, the classroom invites pupils or students to adopt new language patterns or codes, thereby, hopefully, helping them to gain a richer understanding of the world or to become more adept at handling it in action.

In a here and how perspective, such learning as may be achieved through a professional helping dialogue or in a classroom will show through changes in the learner's speech patterns.

Learning mediated through experiential awareness
Terminology: Experiential awareness is mental concept number 2 within the model I'm in the process of explicating. 'Experiential' refers to experiential structures or schemata. The mental contents of such structures or schemata may manifest themselves in purely functional ways, i.e. as parts of a person's cognitive machinery, but without becoming open to conscious scrutiny by that same person. Supplementing 'experiential'

with the term 'awareness' is an indication that I am dealing with mental contents that can be explicitly reflected upon and talked about by its owner.

What kind(s) of learning? Classical experimental psychological studies dealing with problem solving or creativity abound in examples of learning mediated through experiential awareness.[5] Experimental subjects report how, all of a sudden, they somehow, through their mind's eye, 'saw' how a particular problem could be solved (the so-called *Aha-Erlebnis*). Gifted scientists like Einstein likewise describe how answers to scientific riddles that occupy them are suddenly 'there', in the form of an image. Mozart is known as a composer who 'heard' music-to-be-composed, after which followed the long and tedious work of translating it into 'language', i.e., in this case, a musical score. Turning to gloomier matters, such out-of-body experiences as sexually molested children develop as a defense against being psychologically in contact with the molester during the act is an example of a pitiful, but in the circumstances also helpful learning incident, mediated through experiential awareness.

In the earlier subsection I spoke of helping dialogues as a setting making use of languageing as learning medium. Experiential awareness may serve as one means for finding out whether one, or a series of helping dialogues have actually been helpful. The client meets the professional helper in some state of doubt, confusion or the like. She may have notions about what she wants, but is incapable of translating her wishes into action. Helping dialogues may bring about a transformation of her action field (as perceived or imagined) in such a manner that she can now *see her way through,* i.e. has reason to believe that the world will allow her intended action to be carried out successfully.

Learning mediated through bodily action
Terminology: 'Bodily action' signifies 'body in active exchange with environment'. I draw inspiration from George Herbert Mead (1934) whose action concept is a fusion of what he calls *the outer phase of action,* consisting of the patterned interplay between actor and social or non-social objects in the environment, and *the inner phase of action,* consisting of

---

5   Cf., e.g., Duncker, 1945.

activity monitoring programmes rooted in the central nervous system. Extending Mead's terminological usage, I describe learning in the medium of bodily action as a result of a reprogramming of (subsets of) the learner's activity monitoring programmes rooted in his central nervous system.

What kind(s) of learning? Learning in the medium of bodily action shows through changes (of a relatively permanent nature) in the learner's way of practically engaging himself in the world of social and non-social objects surrounding him. A child learning to ride a bicycle needs supporting props when he starts (extra wheels, a grown up's hand), but ends up triumphantly managing himself and his bike all by himself. His body has learnt to control, i.e. to be in fruitful exchange with the bicycle-as-environment.

Another example: As a self-taught amateur fluteplayer, I am aware that my body (fingers, breathing, posture …) is today capable of producing music which, ten or twenty years ago, would have been utterly beyond my reach. Somehow, my body has learned (programmed itself) to do things that, earlier on, were desired but still beyond its reach. Exactly what is learned and how … ? – only the body knows!

The reader may have noticed that both of the above examples deal with learning incidents involving non-social environmental objects. The reasons for this one-sidedness will become clear in the next sub-section.

Learning mediated through social exchange structure
Terminology: Viewing social discourse (languageing), experiential awareness and bodily action as learning facilitating media are fairly mainstream. Viewing social exchange structure in the same manner is more contested. This is illustrated in the field of organizational learning, where certain traditions describe learning as a process essentially belonging to the individual (e.g. Kolb, 1984; Argyris & Schön, 1996), whereas others (Lave & Wenger, 1991) describe social communities as learning subjects.[6]

In the earlier sub-section on bodily action I referred to George Her-

---

6 Authors who in their writing and research practice favour learning as individually mediated will not necessarily, for theoretical reasons, oppose the idea that it may also be conceived as socially mediated. But some do (Haslebo, 1998).

bert Mead. With Darwinism as his main inspirational source, Mead rejected the Descartes-inspired idea that conscious awareness be understood as human psychology's foundational category. Instead he saw bodily action as such a category. Superficially, this move might make him look like a supporter of the radical behaviorist movement launched successfully by Watson some thirteen years before Mead delivered the lectures that became posthumously published as *Mind, Self and Society* (1934). In reality, Mead's rejection of Watson's theoretical stance and research strategy was as firm as his rejection of consciousness-centred psychology. His theoretical disagreement shows in his calling himself a *social* behaviorist. He understands social exchange structures (or *conversations of gestures*) as epistemologically prior to individual bodily action (singular gestures, that gain their potential meaning through the way they are being responded to). In a footnote (1934, p. 130) he makes a distinction between social organisms and individual organisms as follows: "A social organism – that is, a social group of individual organisms – constitutes or creates its own special environment of objects just as, and in the same sense as, an individual organism constitutes or creates its own environment of objects (which, however, is much more rudimentary than the environment constructed by a social organism)."

As yet another means towards grasping my reasons for calling 'social exchange structure' a learning medium, Luhman's (2005) distinction between social systems and psychic systems may be helpful. Social exchange structures depend on persons. Yet such structures also live a life of their own. In social systems 'the communication is communicating'. This communicating communication may be torn apart and analyzed as singular utterances uttered in series, one by one, by singular human individuals (understood as psychic systems). But such a cumulative analysis will not give us a grasp of what the social system is 'doing' – or, possibly, learning.

What kind(s) of learning? As already hinted at in the terminological note, bodily action and social exchange structure as learning media are closely related. When looking at singular learning instances within social settings, it may, generally speaking, be difficult to assign such instances to one learning medium rather than the other. This difficulty is reflected in the fact that, in the above sub-section, my two examples of bodily action mediated learning were both concerned with actions directed towards inanimate objects: a bicycle, a flute. While writing, I did consider several possible examples where one person's actions were directed towards another person or a group of persons. With each and every example I could think of I had to conclude that the learning taking place was doubly mediated, namely both through individual actors' body-based action programmes and through a reprogramming of social exchange structures 'belonging' to a social organism, i.e. to a collective 'we', rather than to any singular actor, or I.

Using the above considerations as background, I shall present the following two examples.

The learning taking place when mother and infant interact is mediated through pattern changes taking place in two bodies *and* pattern changes taking place in the exchange structure distinguishing the dyad. Asking which of the two media has priority and is driving the other is not a constructive question. The two are dialectically linked.

The same may be said about such learning as takes place, e.g., when a close-knit work team receives a new member. Integration of the new member in the team's work routines may, on the one hand, demand that not only he, but possibly also some of the old team members, make adjustments in their bodily rooted action programmes. The changes taking place in the team's way-of-functioning may, however, also be described and analysed as learning reflecting the team's efforts (as social organism) to maintain its structural identity.

In spite of it being difficult, by and large, to make clearcut distinctions between learning mediated through bodily action and through social exchange structure, it seems fairly easy to point at concrete examples where one of the two is activated without the other following suit. This will be illustrated in section 2 below dealing with the learning transfer problem.

2. The problem of learning transfer

Generally speaking, the problem of learning transfer refers to situations where (1) it is hoped or expected that learning acquired within one situational framework will spread to other situational frameworks, but where (2) such spread, or transfer effects, fail to materialize.

Using the terminology introduced in the model of section 1, the problem of learning transfer may be spelled out as follows.

As stated in the very first paragraph of section 1, I tentatively regard the catalogue enumerating four learning media as taxonomic. Until otherwise convinced I shall defend the position that, at the given level of abstraction, the four media cover the learning field.[7] Lack of learning transfer becomes a problem when, contrary to somebody's hopes or expectations, personal learning originating in one medium fails to get translated into learning mediated through one or more among the other three learning media listed.

As in section 1, I shall illustrate my position through examples – starting with some that show lack of learning transfer within the mental category:

Lack of transfer from languageing-mediated learning to learning mediated through experiential awareness: Languageing-mediated learning acquired in the classroom or a professional helping dialogue is hoped to affect the learner's way of viewing his surroundings, but may involve no more than a change of description: The client has learned to speak a new jargon, in line with what his teacher or coach wanted him to. As it happened, the new jargon did not, to any significant degree, become a difference that made any difference – outside the languageing sphere where it was first developed. No interesting change could be observed in his experiential awareness, his bodily actions, his social surroundings.

Lack of transfer from learning mediated through experiential awareness to languageing-mediated learning: Learning mediated through experiential awareness may be hard to put into words, i.e. be more or less ineffable. Mystics often claim that their vision have such qualities. For themselves, this need not represent a problem, given that they attach tremendous learning qualities to the visions 'as they are'. The degree of ineffability clinging to their visions may become problematic in so far as they may

---

7 The taxonomy issue is not theoretically important to me. I introduce it as a way of inviting others to challenge it. I've had discussions with myself as to whether *thinking* should be considered a fifth learning medium. I've made up my mind that, personally, I find it reasonable to view thinking as a learning medium within the mental sphere, but derived from (some combination of) languageing and experiential awareness – meaning that I consider thinking a less basic learning medium than the latter two. Space doesn't allow me to argue more substantially for this viewpoint – but it is certainly one that may be challenged.

wish to transmit their personal learning to others through teaching or preaching.

Next, I bring some example from within the behavioural category.

Lack of transfer from bodily action mediated learning to learning mediated through social exchange structure: In section one, I mentioned the situation where a close-knit work team receives a new member. Such a new member may get the notion that certain work routines (bodily actions), which he himself has learnt in other settings, could make a valuable contribution to the team's work routines. For these reasons he may, as an openly declared strategy or through more devious means, try to have aspects of his own, old routines transferred to or integrated into the team's work related social exchange structure – and he may end up seeing his efforts frustrated. Without it necessarily being put into words, the team demands of its newcomer that he adopts the team's work mores unreservedly without leaving any room for inspirational impact the other way round.

Lack of transfer from learning mediated through social exchange structure to bodily action mediated learning: Bosses in an organization may wish to improve employees' work practices through some kind of structural reshuffling initiated by top-down decree. In some cases such a strategy may work, in others it may fail, depending on employees' readiness to let the new structural constraints get translated into genuine personal learning. Such top-down strategies are bound to fail when employees accept the new structural procedures in no more than a mechanical fashion, otherwise doing their best to carry on with their established work routines as if nothing has happened.

Ending this sub-section I give examples showing lack of learning transfer between mental and behavioural learning media.

Lack of transfer from learning mediated through mental media to socially mediated learning: A large section of the literature dealing with learning is devoted to a critique of the 'scholastic learning paradigm' (e.g. Nielsen & Kvale, 1999). This critique bemoans – among other things – that classroom learning, typically, is narrowly restricted to the mental sphere and fails to get translated to the behavioural sphere. As a possible remedy, it is suggested that mentally mediated learning be supplemented, or supplanted by pragmatically inspired types of learning: learning by doing, apprenticeship training, etc.

Lack of transfer from behaviourally mediated learning to learning mediated through mental media: According to traditional Scientific Management thinking (Taylor, 1911) production workers should be trained exclusively in the bodily action medium. The assembly line required them to do the same simple motions over and over again. It was deemed unnecessary, even potentially disruptive, to have them also reflect (through joint languageing) upon the significance of what they were doing. Today, such narrow training efforts are generally repudiated. It leaves trainees with a very narrow competence field doomed to break down when presented problems don't match the rigid action monitoring programmes that have been installed. "You learn to use a hammer, and the world becomes full of nails!" – but what do you do if the problem at hand is definitely not one that can be dealt with through hammer-and-nails based methods?

The master programme that will be used as case-example in the third and final section was in part created to circumvent this problem of methodological narrowness in the professional field of coaching. Within a fairly brief span of time coaching has become tremendously popular. This has created a huge demand for professional training. Fairly brief training courses based on one singular methodological or theoretical perspective will inevitably lead to a fairly narrow competence field, especially if the trainee brings with him little or no experience in the field of professional communication. The master programme is meant to engage students in a study programme of two years' duration in an academic setting. The programme, however, includes activities that, traditionally, will more often be found in non-academic educational programmes – which is what makes the master programme interesting in the context of the present paper.

3. How to circumvent the learning transfer problem

Learning theorists are often concerned with trying to find out which learning medium should be considered the basic one, i.e. the one driving the others.

The history of modern academic psychology is full of examples. Let me just introduce three.

John B. Watson's famous battle cry (1913), inaugurating the era of hard core behaviourism, has already been referred to. In it, Watson denounced experiential awareness as learning medium on the grounds that it was intractable to rigorous scientific research. Instead, and with great success in terms of gaining followers, he made a case for (a very simplistic notion of) bodily action as the only scientifically respectable learning medium. Nearly half a century later, Watson's equally hard core colleague, Skinner, wrote his book on *Verbal behavior* (1957) aimed at proving that languageing-based learning could be understood as a sub-variety of (an even more simplistic version of) bodily action-based learning. One other brilliant learning researcher, Tolman (1961), with a fondness for running rats in learning mazes at least equalling Watson's and Skinner's, invented the term cognitive maps. Doing this, he came as close to reintroducing experiential awareness as a functional learning medium as rat-based psychology would allow.

Earlier in this paper, I have likewise referred to the discussion among organizational learning theorists as to whether individually mediated (bodily action, experiential awareness) or socially mediated (languageing, social exchange structures) should be given theoretical priority.[8] One experience that has concretely inspired me to write this paper is that social constructionism is often presented as a viewpoint favouring languageing-based learning as the 'mother of all learning'.[9]

The present paper is emphatically in favour of a viewpoint saying that, generally speaking, no natural hierarchy exists between the four learning media (with consequential learning modes) enumerated through the section one model. Given the proper circumstances (setting) and timing they all have the capacity to function as learning initiating and learning supporting vehicles. There are no good theoretical reasons to prioritize one rather than another as being 'the best' or most basic. Also worth considering is the fact that talents for making use of one medium rather than another are not evenly distributed, neither among students nor teachers.

The strategic recommendation entailed by the above viewpoint is that designers of teaching and learning processes should make an effort

---

8   Cf. footnote 2.
9   I do not find such a viewpoint warranted in authoritative texts on social constructionism (e.g. Gergen & Gergen, 2004). It seems to arise as a mechanical effect of academic discourse patterns coining arguments in terms of mutually negating opposites: "If my theory is right, other theories within the same reality domain must be wrong, or at least less right."

to include a wide variety of media, rather than few, in learning events, thereby allowing to students the possibility of, first, locating, then following their own preferred learning style.

In the following sub-sections I will illustrate how designers behind a recently inaugurated Master programme of Organizational Coaching (MOC) have let themselves be guided by such a strategy of learning media variation.

Four learning arenas: Auditorium, Laboratory, Practicum and Reflection
The formal presentation of the master programme states that "(t)he master programme is designed as a combination of classroom teaching (Auditorium), training activities (Laboratory), and practical experimentation (Practicum) connecting reflection with action."

Auditorium, Laboratory, Practicum and personal Reflection we understand as four distinct learning arenas each offering its own unique contribution to the programme whole. Below I shall describe the four arenas separately, at the same time specifying the way each makes privileged use of one of the learning media presented in the section 1-model above.

Auditorium is the classroom. Already in section 1, I described the traditional classroom as a setting favouring languageing as learning medium. Hence, I need not elaborate this point much further. Much can be done (role playing, discussion groups, etc.) in order to add variety to the old-style classroom languageing form consisting of one-way communication from talking teacher to listening students. As teachers in the MOC-programme we make use of such variety while still honouring the academic lecture, supplemented with discussion, as a valid, languageing-based vehicle for learning.

Laboratory is the arena for personal, practical training. The Laboratory arena has bodily action as its privileged learning medium. One special feature of MOC is that its very title focuses on one specific professional helping dialogue, namely that of (organizational) coaching. As has been emphasized in section 1, the privileged learning medium offered by a coaching session *to the coachee* is that of languageing. Languageing, however, is only of limited value to the coach moving towards practical mastery of the complexities of the coaching dialogue. Just like the child experimenting with his bicycle, or me experimenting with my flute, the coach must allow her body to find its own way. Her body may have action preferences that do not match her theoretical preferences acquired in the classroom. Her body may teach her things about coaching, dialogue, human encounters, etc., that no amount of languageing, however clever and theoretically refined, could possibly have made her understand.

Practicum is a learning arena requiring that the student moves outside the classroom. Practicum activities make use of action research methods for instructional purposes. With increasing intensity as the master programme progresses students are invited to take on the role of action researchers in their own workplace-organizations.[10] When recruiting students we make it clear that, ideally speaking, we conceive of their workplace-organizations as programme participants. In their third semester, students are not evaluated on the basis of a written project report. Instead they will present the results of an action research project, documented in three ways, as follows:

1) An edited process log allowing each student to make personal-professional reflections concerning her difficulties, successes, choices along the way ... ;
2) A text written for persons or group(s) somehow involved in the project – testing the student's ability as a competent, professional communicator;
3) An oral presentation in a conference setting, likewise testing her communicative ability, but now directed towards a professional community of peers.

We see this Practicum design component as our master programme's most ambitious effort to circumvent the learning transfer problem. Given the link between Practicum and action research, social exchange structure is the learning medium most significantly involved in the master programme's Practicum activities.

Last, but not least, we regard personal *Reflection* as a fourth learning arena at the disposal of our students. Personal Reflection uses experiential awareness as a privileged learning medium. Personal Reflection is present in the three learning arenas mentioned above. Thus personal Reflection is what hopefully may create a unity out of the diverse learning experiences the student encounters as a participant in Auditorium, Laboratory, Practicum.

---

10 Cf. Coghlan & Brannick, 2005

4. Concluding remarks

Learning has many faces and may be conceptualised along a variety of theoretical dimensions. This article has dealt with four media through which individual and social learning processes may be channelized: languageing, experiential awareness, bodily action, and social exchange structure. Apart from describing each learning facilitating medium, the article has defended the theoretical position that each medium should be considered valuable in its own right, and that the four media are not tied together by any 'natural' hierarchy of importance.

In the article's third section I have described how this theoretical position has left its mark on a master programme in organizational coaching. In the programme design explicit care has been taken to make room for a variety of learning (and teaching) arenas matching the learning media variety described in the paper – as is shown in figure 2.

Figure 2: Match (in MOC) between learning arenas and learning media

Learning arena	Favoured learning medium
Auditorium	**Languageing**
Laboratory	**Bodily action**
Practicum	**Social exchange structure**
Reflection	**Experiential awareness**

The described design features imply that the master programme acquires an instructional profile diverging from what is habitually found in academic educational settings. Nothing academically peculiar attaches to our way of using languageing and personal reflection as learning media. The weight accorded to bodily action as learning medium (Laboratory activities) hints at a resemblance to crafts apprenticeship. We are fully aware that social science students may be invited to set up or participate in delimited research projects employing action research methods (social exchange structure as learning medium). Yet we do believe that our large-scale employment of action research inspired Practicum activities is fairly unique.[11]

---

11 Documentation for this belief may be found in Willert, 2009.

References

Argyris, C. & Schön, D. (1996) *Organizational Learning II*. New York: Addison-Wesley

Coghlan, D. & Brannick, T. (2005) *Doing Action research in Your Own Organization*. London: Sage

Duncker, K. (1945) Problem Solving. *Psychological Monographs, 58, 5*.

Gergen, K.J. & Gergen, M. (2004) *Social construction – entering the dialogue*. Chagrin Fall (Ohio): Taos Institute Publications

Haslebo, G. (1998) *Konsultation i organisationer. (Consultation in Organizations)* Copenhagen: Dansk Psykologisk Forlag

Kolb, D.A. (1984) *Experiential Learning*. Englewood Cliffs (N.J.): Prentice-Hall

Lave, J. & Wenger, E. (1991) *Situated Learning*. New York: Cambridge University Press

Luhmann, N. (2005) *Sociale systemer. (Social Systems)*. København: Hans Reitzels forlag

Mead, G.H. (1934) *Mind, Self and Society*. Chicago: University of Chicago Press.

Nielsen, K. & Kvale, S. (1999) *Mesterlære. Læring som social praksis. (Apprenticeship: Learning as social practice)*. Copenhagen: Hans Reitzels forlag

Pearce, W.B. (2007) *Kommunikation og skabelsen af sociale verdener. (Communication and the making of social worlds)*. Copenhagen: Dansk Psykologisk Forlag.

Skinner, B.F. (1957) *Verbal behavior*. New York: Appleton-Century-Crofts

Taylor, F. (1911) *Principles of Scientific Management*. New York: Harper & Brothers.

Tolman, E.C. (1927) A Behaviorist's definition of consciousness. *Psychological Review, 34*

Watson, J.B. (1913) Psychology as the behaviorist views it. *Psychological Review, 20*.

Willert, S. (2009) Uddannelse af organisatoriske coaches – et pædagogisk ambitiøst masterprogram (Training organizational coaches – a pedagogically ambitious master programme). In: Nørlem, J. (ed.) *Coachingens landskaber (Coaching landscapes)*. Copenhagen: Hans Reitzels forlag.

Towards a Substantial Notion of Validation

Christina Chaib & Ingela B. Prulovic

Introduction

Our study concerns the pervasive concept of validation of knowledge and competencies extensively used in Sweden and in Europe today. "The activity/process that makes the individual's knowledge and competence visible is called 'validering' (validation) in Swedish" (Anderson, Fejes & Ahn, 2004, p 2), and different concepts are applied in different countries (ibid.). Already in the 1980 one used Prior Experiental Learning-PEL in USA, and in UK later on Assessment (or Accreditation) of Prior Experiental Learning, APEL. Validation is the French concept for APEL. Connecting to the Adult Education Initiative (AEI) in 1996 RPL[12] was introduced in Sweden (SOU 1996:27).

In 1996 the OECD formulated a strategy to make lifelong learning a reality for all. This included the creation of new instruments for validation of knowledge and competencies. The European commission supported this strategy for lifelong learning in a year 2000 memorandum that stressed the need for a lifelong learning strategy to promote active citizenship, increased employment, and mobility within Europe (Memorandum, 2000). The strategy is expected to facilitate the development of systems and methods that are acceptable to workplaces and institutions and that include and promote education and competencies as necessary tools for development. Strategies and methods for validation have since been extensively developed and tested in the European arena.

Within the European Universities Continuing Education Network, EUCEN, Sweden, together with 24 European countries, is engaged in

---

12 APL – accreditation of prior learning, APEL – accreditation for prior experiential learning, PLA – prior learning assessment, RPL – recognition of prior learning.

a project called Observal to gather information, scrutinize validation processes and review different texts about validation. In our view, validation, both as a concept and as a phenomenon, lacks a common interpretation among professionals working with validation, regardless of the country in which they work.

There are many reasons why an individual might want to be submitted to validation, such as being at risk for losing a job, wanting a new job, beginning or returning to study, or even to obtain a higher income. We have observed that sometimes the initiative to validate candidates comes from industry, especially when a certain job has low status. We are concerned in our study with the question of whether all these experiences/processes really can or should be identified and labelled as validation.

The aim of our study is to conduct a critical analysis of validation as a concept and as a phenomenon. In the text we will present two different processes of validation, interpret them and finally, relate them to the Swedish official definition of validation. One of the main questions for our study is whether it is reasonable to suppose that validation is/can/should be a solution to many kinds of problems within the broad field of assessing and valuing competencies, or rather, do we need more sophisticated concepts for a more robust validation?

Lifelong learning and validation

Validation is put forth as a "delivering" solution in different national strategies and policy documents within various political fields such as employment, integration, education and social welfare. Mentioned, among other things, are strategies for increased mobility and a well-functioning labour market. In this perspective, two concepts turn out to be central: lifelong learning and validation.

The strategy formulated in 1996 by the OECD-countries' ministries of education was meant to create and enhance instruments for validation of knowledge and competencies. In its memorandum of 2000, the European commission expressed the need for an overarching strategy to carry out a plan for lifelong learning. To stimulate mobility within Europe, systems and methods for the recognition of education and competencies are needed. These are to be adopted by workplaces and institutions in the European countries.

A lifelong learning perspective entails that various actors, such as individuals, society and the labour market share the responsibility for education and competence development. Throughout their lives, individuals need current knowledge and competences in order to adapt to the demands of society and of the labour market. These competences can be required in traditional learning settings as well as in the workplace or in everyday situations. The phenomenon of assessing and evaluating different types of competences is rather new, becoming commonplace only about a decade ago. The meaning of 'validation', therefore, is rather unstable, changing over time and from person to person.

Previously, validation was applied in order to assess competences that were not defined or captured by any existing documents (Skolverket, 1999, The Swedish Agency of Education). The definition of validation initially used by Skolverket was: "assessment and recognition of skills and competences that have been achieved outside the formal educational system" (Skolverket, 1999, p. 9, from SOU 1997:158, our translation). The following year validation was understood somewhat differently. The Swedish national initiative on competence development for adults, the Adult Education Initiative (AEI) spanning the period of 1997-2002, adopted the following definition (ibid., p. 9, from SOU 1998:51):

> To validate means to identify real competence and to describe it in such a way that the stakeholders – industry and educational providers (adult education, higher education etc.) – can accept the description. (Our translation.)

Both the government at that time and AEI declared that assessment and validation have a broad meaning and signification (ibid. p. 9).

> By validation is meant a structural assessment and recognition, a valuing of skills and competences that have been achieved both inside and outside the formal educational system. Another way of expressing this is to say that validation is the measuring and recognition, in a formalized way, of real competence or tacit knowledge. (Our translation.)

In the 1999 definition used by Skolverket, a lifelong learning perspective is evident. Validation is "assessment of competences and skills the adult person has acquired through studies, in social life, in working life, both in formal and informal ways" (ibid., p. 10, our translation).

The official definition of validation used today is from the Department of Education, and reads as follows (Ds 2003:23, p. 19):

> Validation is a process that means a structured assessment, estimation, documentation and acceptance of knowledge and competencies that a person has independently of how it has been acquired.

Validation aims at assessing the individual's real competence, wherever or whenever it might have been acquired – in Sweden or abroad, recently or a long time ago. This perspective corresponds to how the concepts are normally used by Cedefop (The European Centre for the Development of Vocational Training). Through validation, the competencies an individual has acquired are surveyed and documented. These encompass formal, non-formal and informal learning. Informal learning occurs as an incidental result of different activities in work or everyday life. According to the former Validation Authority, validation is of vital importance in three different contexts in particular:

- in ongoing studies aimed at describing or identifying a person's level of knowledge, to adapt the content of or shorten a course of studies;
- in connection with supervision aiming at identifying a relevant education program for an individual; and
- to document real competencies and skills prior to employment or in connection with staff development.

Validation is a phenomenon found in all sectors of society, and is more or less subject to different ideological and even theoretical approaches. According to the Validation Authority, the concept of validation causes confusion because it is also used for other types of phenomena that have existed for a long time and that extend beyond the intended scope of validation (Delrapport från valideringsdelegationen, 2006). There is a difference between validation, which is about the valuation and confirmation of knowledge, and testing, which is about verification of competencies related to a job in a specific vocational or academic field (ibid. p. 4; from SOU 2001:78).

Recent overview

In recent years, with the requirement to carry out validation, much has been published on the topic. The texts have had various purposes and target groups and have helped people engaged in validation to better understand what validation is about. Of these many publications, we mention authors such as Fejes and Andersson (2005), Lundborg (2005), Andersson (2006), Andersson and Hult (2008), Lindvall (2004) and Gustavsson and Mouwitz (2008). The final report from the Delegation of Validation provides many different perspectives of validation and makes recommendations regarding relevant activities.

Below, as current examples of work in the field, we briefly describe two studies on validation representing different arenas:

The first example, from the field of Liberal Adult Education, describes a model or concept developed in order to enhance individuals' self-esteem and self-confidence (Valideringsdelegationen, 2007). The learning that takes place in various sorts of non-profit organizations is referred to as general competencies and is seldom measured or evaluated, thus remaining invisible. An essential aim of this validation process is that course participants develop a deeper awareness of their own competencies, since such awareness may increase both self-esteem and self-confidence. Moreover, increased self-esteem and self-confidence may enable individuals to better describe and present their personal competencies in a written document.

The second example, reported by Schultz and Sandberg (2007), describes the process and results of a project called Validus, conducted in cooperation between the Universities of Linköping and Lund and various trade unions. The project focused on validation of non-formal and informal learning about workplace environment and workplace rights (in relation to three particular post-secondary courses) acquired by workers through work-place learning. The main purpose was to "develop a general model with flexible solutions for validation of knowledge acquired through work-place learning" (ibid., p. 2). The participants appreciated the opportunity to earn credits toward higher education entrance requirements as well as a written document certifying their knowledge. Some criticism, however, was directed toward the fact that the assessment in the validation model was dependent on the teacher/course coordinator's way of understanding and interpreting knowledge and competence. The authors suggest that there is a discrepancy between the way academics understand knowledge gained through formal study and knowledge gained informally or non-formally.

Aim of the study

The aim of the empirical study presented in this paper is to illuminate the wide range of approaches to or understanding of validation. In search of a substantial notion of validation, we intend to look at how the concept as well as the phenomenon of validation is used.

We have chosen to investigate and analyze two different validation processes focusing our analysis on three aspects of the validations. The first deals with the validation process itself, concerning both its conceptualization and its methodology. The second relates to the intentions and reasons why the validations were initiated and represents a societal perspective. Finally, the third focus deals with the intended benefit(s) of validation for the participants. The following questions are to be answered:

What are the intentions/motivations behind and the purposes of the validation processes?

How can we characterize each of the validation studies in terms of how they are conceptualized and in terms of the methodologies used?

What are the benefits to the individuals submitted to the validation?

Sampling and data collection

In the Observal project, each partner country is expected to collect and deliver data on validation to a European database. Our own work in Sweden is done together with a "national working advisory group". The work is conducted within Encell (www.encell.se), a national competence centre for lifelong learning at the University of Jönköping. Observal does not seek only good examples of validation; even the poor or peculiar ones, from which much can be learned, are worth considering. The purpose is to include a broad spectrum of information on the field of validation that will serve as a resource for professionals interested in validation.

We are collecting case studies of validation processes. For this paper we have chosen two cases representing different fields and varying in other ways. Both cases deal with validation of non-formal and informal learning. The first case is within the field of restaurant and large-scale household cooking and the validation concerns an individual. The second case concerns multiple subjects: employees at a workplace within a specific technical industry in Sweden.

We gathered most of the data through interviews. In the first case, we interviewed the counsellor involved, one of the teachers, and the subject of validation, whom we will call Anna. We also observed while Anna was tested/examined in the kitchen, and we reviewed various documents such as her CV, relevant former and current course curricula, and transcripts (credits/grades) of her earlier studies. The data for the second case we collected through one interview with the person responsible for the development and coordination of the validation. This person represents the particular industrial sector at large and not a specific workplace.

The analysis

The analysis of the gathered data was done in two steps. In the first step we have combined the data from the different sources into narratives. We have chosen not to refer to the documents or to the persons interviewed, in order to preserve the flow of the story. We retained the terms and concepts used by the interviewed persons in order to better understand their points of view.

Based upon the outcomes of a cross analysis, we then answer the three research questions. In order to capture the diversity in the data, we highlight similarities and differences in each question.

Results

This chapter is divided into two parts. In the first part we present the two cases. In the second part we answer the three research questions, emphasizing the most salient similarities and differences between the two cases.

Presentation of two cases

The first case, of Anna, is a validation of non-formal and informal learning within the field of restaurant and large-scale household cooking.

Anna had left school toward the beginning of a two-year education programme in this field, and since then the programme has changed significantly. Since leaving school, Anna has been working in the restaurant sector. She has been offered temporary employment in a municipal preschool kitchen. In order for her to secure a permanent position, her employer wants her to complete her restaurant education. There is a vocational training programme organized by a municipal adult education body, based on national courses from the upper secondary school programme; the validation related to these required national courses. Anna's short-term goals were to complete her restaurant education, to obtain formal credit/grades toward the national courses, and to secure permanent employment. She also wanted to be able to work half time while completing a validation process that included a course of study. Her long-term goal was to qualify to enter higher (post-secondary) education. Anna met with a career counsellor, who mapped out her educational and work background. The counsellor identified Anna's goals and related them to institutional, structural, economic and individual conditions. The mapping process revealed that Anna had extensive experience gained through work. After the mapping process, Anna met the teachers for an in-depth interview. The purpose of the interview was to yield a first estimation of the number of practical and theoretical requirements Anna would be able to validate. The investigation indicated that Anna would be able to validate national courses corresponding to at least 1.000 credits, amounting to one year of full time study. To obtain credit toward all required courses in the two-year vocational training programme, Anna would need to continue with the validation process and complete further training/coursework. A course of study combined with a continuing validation process was planned in accordance with her individual abilities and goals. The validation process contained interviews, written assignments and various assigned tasks designed to allow her to exhibit her competence in different job situations and thus, to enable teachers to validate her experiences and competencies towards the curriculum of several courses. Anna achieved her short-term goal of securing a permanent position and is now on her way to achieve her longer-term goal. The individual course of study developed for her as the result of the validation process meant a shortened length of study (one year instead of two) and fewer study loans. Other benefits were her increased awareness of her competencies and abilities, and thus increased self-esteem. The validation process made it possible for Anna to combine simultaneous validation, supplementary training and half-time employment.

The second case also focuses on validation of non-formal and informal learning, but at the workplace. Here, the validation concerns competencies of the employees, with reference to specific vocational competencies controlled and required by the trade union of the specific industrial sector. The main purpose of the validation is to identify "hidden gaps in competencies", to establish individual descriptions of each employee's competencies, and to develop individual plans for competence development within the scope of a "bridging programme" that offers employees a means of making up for gaps in their individual profiles. The validation is also to be used as a tool for recruitment. The company initiates the validation, from a perspective of company needs, and the validation focuses on the "status" of an individual's employability. The validation process is divided into one theoretical session, carried out by representatives of an employers' association of the specific industrial sector, and one practical session. The theoretical session employs a specific web-based tool called Exerciser, developed by vocational experts and containing 3000 questions corresponding to the vocational requirements of nine different professions within the given industrial sector. The candidate must answer ten randomly selected questions from each section of relevance to him/her. Results are expressed in percentage terms to enable comparisons between different sections of questions and also to inform the candidates of their achievement levels. The practical sessions are carried out at the companies where the candidates are employed, at a time that is suitable for the companies. On these occasions, one representative from the relevant profession surveys the candidate as he or she performs the practical activities upon which the practical validation is based.

Once the theoretical and practical sessions of validation are completed, the results are compiled in a description of competencies for each candidate. These are then reported to the leaders of the validation at the industry association. In the next step, these leaders report the results to the leaders of the actual company where the candidates are employed, as well as to representatives of the relevant trade unions. The final step is to inform the candidates of their individual outcomes. With reference to these, an individual plan for competence development is created for each employee wherein missing competencies are identified. Based on the written document, the candidates join a bridging programme covering the missing competencies. One benefit of the validation, according to the person interviewed, is less faulty production caused by lack of knowledge. The validation leads to higher efficiency in the companies. The individual descriptions of competencies function as a tool for quality assurance for the company and promote increased self-esteem among the candidates. The outcomes of the validation are also used as tools for rewarding the employees, who may be granted salary increases upon their completion of supplementary training. Another benefit mentioned by companies is that they have been able to reduce the amount of time spent conversing with their staffs about competence development. The process is also seen to minimize the risk of subjective assessment/judgment on the part of senior staff, as they discuss competence development or salary with their employees.

Answers to research questions

In this section, we will highlight the most important differences and similarities between the cases. Since the research questions overlap somewhat in scope, there will be some overlap in the answers as well.

Which are the intentions/motivations behind and the purposes of these validation processes?
The differences in purpose between these two cases are related to the subjects taking part in the process of validation. In the first case, validation is described as a tool for identifying a single individual's competencies acquired through work and relating these competencies to national curricula. In the second case, validation is described as a tool for identifying "hidden gaps in competencies" among company staff. There is a difference between identifying competencies and identifying lack of, or gaps in competencies. The first case focuses on the possibility for an individual, Anna, to reach specific personal goals under conditions acceptable to her. Validation in the second case was motivated by the desire to create an effective means of developing staff competency and was aimed at verification of employees' specific competencies in accordance with company expectations or requirements. Furthermore, here validation is used to support the recruitment process.

The validation in case one is carried out within the scope of public services, with the individual's needs in focus. The validation in case two is carried out with the specific industry association's need in focus. In the first case, an individual seeks to secure permanent employment, while the target group of the second case consists only of employed persons.

How can we characterize, for each case, the conceptualization of and the methodology used in the validation?
The answer to this second question deals with how validation is understood and interpreted as a phenomenon. The way validation is understood and interpreted affects the methods used and the procedure of the validation process.

The organisation behind the validation of Anna interpreted validation as a means for her to obtain formal credit toward national curricula. The individual in this case is expected to have gained experience and knowledge through work that may be equivalent to the course content of the vocational training she hopes to complete. The organisation behind the validation in case two has interpreted validation as a test of knowledge according to specific vocational competence requirements and as a tool to be used in staff development.

In both cases, we have found an intention to relate current competencies to specific requirements: to formal courses in case one, or to specific vocational competence requirements in case two. Competencies that were considered irrelevant to the job were not identified in case two.

In terms of the procedures and methods used, we can also observe differences between the two cases. In the first case the validation begins with a mapping process carried out as an open, investigative dialogue: The organiser has no knowledge of the person or her educational and work background. In the second case no mapping process takes place in the beginning because the organiser is focusing on the company's own staff who are expected to have knowledge relevant to their work. This validation starts with a test of knowledge, which the interviewed person calls validation, and results in a description of competencies.

In both cases, the validation includes an aspect of control, or verification. In case one this is related to national curricula, and in case two to specific competence requirements. In the second case the testing used and the practical sessions are designed to verify the presence and also, significantly, to reveal the absence of specific knowledge required, but not to identify hidden knowledge; that is, they are designed to identify lack of knowledge. There is a clear difference between these two ways of identifying competences: one seeks to identify existing competence and the other, lack of competence. In the first case, the identification of knowledge makes it possible to find hidden knowledge, so that the individual may validate several national curricula; even if gaps in competency are found it is not the main purpose of the validation to find them.

In both cases discussed, the validation results in some sort of supplementary education. In the first case, the individual begins a course of study while the validation is carried out with specific tasks. In the second case, employees receive plans for competence development and they need to participate in a "bridging programme" to make up for gaps in competencies. A big difference between the two cases is that in the first case, it is the individual who chooses to participate in validation and embark upon a course of study, while in the second case, validation and further competence development are imposed upon the employees.

What are the benefits to the individuals submitted to the validation?

The answer to this question concerns not only the benefits to individuals submitted to validation but also, in the second case, to industry. We have observed that it can be difficult to separate benefits from outcomes, as they are integrated phenomena.

In the first case the candidate obtained formal credit toward national curricula and completed her vocational training. This is an outcome related to the purpose of the validation. In the longer term, outcomes connected with the needs of the individual include permanent employment, strengthened possibility to go on to study in higher education, shortened length of time for the current study-route, smaller study-loan, awareness of her own abilities and competences and increased self-esteem. In the second case, the description of each employee's competencies and identification of hidden gaps in competencies are outcomes for the company directly related to the main purpose of the validation. Indirect results for the company include less faulty production, higher efficiency, and validation as a tool for recruitment, quality assurance, and reduction of time-consuming conversations with staff. Another outcome is that, through the description of competencies and subsequent competence development, employees strengthened their employability while possibly experiencing increased self-esteem and pride in their professions. It seems in both cases as if the supplementary education or competence development are outcomes of validation. The validations combined with education result in increased self-esteem and awareness of competence and abilities on the part of the individuals.

Some reflections

In this section we reflect upon some of the differences in approach to/ understanding of validation. We begin here with a look at the Swedish national definition of validation and how it has been interpreted in the two cases.

Again, the official definition used today, from the Swedish Department of Education (Ds 2003:23, p. 19):

> Validation is a process that means a structured assessment, estimation, documentation and acceptance of knowledge and competencies that a person has independently of how it has been acquired.

Central concepts used in the national definition of validation are *assessment, estimation, recognition and documentation*. How is validation in the two cases related to this definition?

The initial phase of the validation in case one consists of a mapping exercise, although the national definition mentions no mapping process. In this case, the organiser makes an assessment of the knowledge the individual has acquired through education and work experience in relation to national curricula. A plan for validation and an individualized study route for supplementary training are created. The documentation of knowledge consists directly of formal grades/credits and this is also a kind of recognition of knowledge.

The validation in case two consists primarily in a test of current knowledge, aiming at discovering lack of knowledge. Together with the description of required competence, the validation contains activities of assessments, estimation and documentation (i.e., of test results). Recognition of competencies here consists in the results of the validation. Since the validation shows hidden gaps in competencies, supplementary training is planned, here called competence development, and leads to the need for supplementary documentation (of newly achieved competencies).

When we analysed the two cases in relation to the national definition of validation, we found that the definition does not include either the mapping process nor the supplementary training or competence development. It seems that validation functions in both the cases as a tool for the organisers to use in determining the level and kind of supplementary training or competence development needed.

Differences in understanding validation
Initially, we found a big difference between the two cases concerning the *interpretation* of 'validation'. There seems to be an ideological/intentional difference between identifying competencies and identifying gaps in competencies. We believe that this difference of interpretation of the meaning of validation depends on or is related to the intentions/motivations behind the validation (i.e., why the validations were initiated). It seems that the two organisations interpret the concept so that it will correspond to their own purposes. While the first organisation, municipal adult education, is primarily concerned with the individual's needs, the second organisation's main concern is the needs of the company. Discussing the contexts of validation, Andersson and Fejes (2005) point to two specific perspectives: system adjustment (systemanpassning) and system change (systemförändring). A system adjustment perspective is characterized by the attempt to be as effective as possible concerning recruitment of students, to get "the right man at the right place" in workplaces and to take into account different kinds of vocational competencies. A system change perspective, on the other hand, is about providing fair opportunities for individuals and being prepared to change the system in order to expand possibilities for development (ibid., p. 172). Gustafsson and Mouwitz (2008) focus on the importance of a point of view of fairness to adult persons who are subjected to validation, emphasizing that people submitted to validation can experience the conditions of validation as uncomfortable. They write (p. 38):

> The adult has also in practice demonstrated both to himself and others competence in handling life and work, but in the validation situation can

easily appear as incompetent, not least in those cases where validation focuses primarily on what the individual *does not know* and *cannot perform.*

We have seen that the way validation is understood affects the purpose and the procedures in a validation process, as well as the target group.

Both cases describe the acceptance of knowledge and real competences as having been achieved upon the completion of supplementary training. This is interesting, as the official definition mentions nothing about supplementary training. Validation is supposed to assess, estimate, document and accept the knowledge and competence a person *has acquired*. Accordingly, validation should result in a document describing the knowledge and competence the person has *already* acquired, and not that which is supposed to be acquired.

The delegation for validation (Final Report, 2008) stresses that it should be possible for a person to receive a certificate, a description, and not just grades or credits. The document ought to have a status of legitimacy, and be understandable to various stakeholders. It is not necessary for a person to sign up for supplementary training when validation is carried out within the field of municipal adult education.

If we look at current debates surrounding validation we notice that validation is sometimes seen as a way to increase staff competency. In our view, validation should recognize the competence a person has already acquired. To increase the level of competence, supplementary training is planned, as we have seen in the two cases.

If we regard acceptance of knowledge and competences from another perspective, as the former Validation Authority does, we can see that acceptance is a vital part of validation. If we reflect upon benefits for the individual, such as increased awareness of abilities and competences and increased self-esteem, as an effect of validation, we can see another aspect of what is vital to validation. In one of the reports written by the Validation Authority, guidance is seen as an orienting, investigative part of the process with the purpose of encouraging the individual's self-awareness and self-understanding (Valideringsdelegationen, 2004, p. 8). According to many practitioners in the field of Liberal Adult Education, this may be one of the most essential aims of the validation process, namely, that individuals develop awareness of their own competencies. Self-esteem and enhanced self-confidence can result in a better ability to describe and present one's personal competencies (Valideringsdelegationen, 2007).

Validation – a broad concept
How can validation as a concept be understood? That is, what is the proper extension of the term 'validation'? We have seen several definitions as the definition has developed over time. In the definition formulated by the Committee of Competence Development for Adults, or Kunskapslyftet (Skolverket, 1999, p. 9), we find the interpretation of validation as meaning *to identify real competence.* The word *identify* is no longer current in the official definition of today. In Kunskapslyftet's definition, stakeholders, such as *industry and educational providers (adult education, higher education)*, are included. In the official definition of today, no stakeholders are specified. As the definition of validation has changed over time, we have observed that the interpretation of the concept of validation differs. In the earlier definition, Kunskapslyftet's (ibid.), it is specified that we are talking about real competence. This is lost in the definition of today. It has not been our intention in this paper to clarify the meaning of validation but rather, to highlight the current lack of clarity on the subject. We think that it is important that the discussion continues.

One might think that validation includes many different "activities" and can be a solution to many problems. The varying interpretations of validation affect both the purpose for which and the methodology with which it is used. We believe that it is not reasonable to regard validation as a solution to all sorts of different problems within the field of assessing and valuing competencies; rather, it ought to be reserved as a solution to only some of these problems. There exist other phenomena within this field that have been confused with validation due to their similarities of purpose or expected outcomes. We also think that too generous an interpretation of validation hinders its original purpose.

References

Andersson, Per & Fejes, Andreas, (2005). *Kunskapers värde – validering i teori och praktik.* Lund: Studentlitteratur. (The Values of Knowledge – Validation in Theory and Practice)

Andersson, Per (2006). Validering av vuxnas lärande (Validation of adults' learning). In S. Larsson & L.-E. Olsson (Red.) *Om vuxnas studier* (About adults' studies). Lund: Studentlitteratur.

Andersson, Per & Hult, Åsa (2008). *Validation in the Nordic Countries. Policy and*

Practice. Nordic Network for Adult Learning, NVL. ISBN 978-91-976112-3-7
Delrapport från Valideringsdelegationen. (A report from the Delegation of Validation). 2006-12-15. Dnr: VLD2006/81.5. www.valideringsdelegationen.se
Final Report (2008). The Final Report from the Delegation of Validation. Towards a National Structure. *(Valideringsdelegationens slutrapport. Mot en nationell struktur.)*
Gustavsson, Lars & Mouwitz, Lars (2008). *Validation of adults' proficiency – fairness in focus.* National Center for Mathematics Education, NCM, University of Gothenburg.
Lindvall, Eva (2004). *Vägledning i validering: att resa i livstiden* (Guidance in validation: to travel in lifetime). Lund: Studentlitteratur.
Lundborg, Inge Marie (2005). Validering - ett sätt att värdera och erkänna kunskap (Validation – a way of assessing and recognizing knowledge). In C. G. Wenestam & B. Lendahls Rosendahl (Red.). *Lärande i vuxenlivet* (Learning as adult). Lund: Studentlitteratur.
Memorandum (2000). *Memorandum om livslångt lärande (Memorandum of Lifelong Learning).*
Schultz, Linda & Sandberg, Fredrik (2007). *Validus II – Report from step 2 of a cooperation project concerning validation of union trade work knowledge acquired through work-place learning.* FoV Rapport. No 13. University of Lund, Sweden.
SOU 2001:78. *Validering av vuxnas kunskap och kompetens.* (Validation of Knowledge and Competencies Among Adults). Stockholm: Utbildningsdepartementet.
Skolverket (1999), (The Swedish National Agency for Education). *Validering* (Validation). ISBN 91-89313-70-4
Validering m m. – fortsatt utveckling av vuxnas lärande. (Ds 2003:23). (Validation et cetera – an ongoing Development of Adults' Learning). Stockholm: Utbildningsdepartementet.
Valideringsdelegationen (2007). Concept for Validation of General Competencies in Adult Education (e.g. folk high schools) and Informal Learning. (*Koncept för validering av generella kompetenser i folkbildning och informellt lärande*). Dnr: VLD 2007/56.
Valideringsdelegationen. (2004). *Validering en institutionaliserad genväg.* Dnr: VLD 2004/24 5. Valideringsdelegationens kansli., Norrköping. www.valideringsdelegationen.se

Initial education and training of adult teachers and trainers in Denmark

Anne Larson and Marcella Milana

Introduction[13]

Denmark has a long tradition for education and training for adults. In 1765, Green held a course in Copenhagen for craftsmen on topics within both science and liberal arts. Green, however, was not the first to offer education to adults. Since the time of the reformation, Christian education had targeted adults as well as children and young people. In 1844, the first folk high school in Denmark was established by a group of people including Grundtvig. The aim of the folk high school was a combination of liberal education stressing the national aspect, and vocationally oriented education related to the agricultural sector. The nineteenth century was also the century when the first evening schools for adults saw the light. The first evening classes were established in the country, but later spread to the cities. They were followed by evening classes arranged by the bourgeoisie and later by the labour movement. (Korsgaard, 1997).

Like the first folk high school combined liberal and vocationally oriented education, it is difficult to make a clear distinction between the history of general and vocationally oriented adult education in Denmark. In 1958, the first technical preparatory courses aimed at young people and adults were established in Denmark. The courses were the forerunners of the later adult education centres offering general adult education at secondary school level. The establishment of the technical preparatory courses was part of an overall strategy for development

---

13 Parts of the paper have earlier been published as a chapter in Milana & Larson (2009). *Becoming Adult Educators in the Nordic Baltic Region: National Report: Denmark*. Copenhagen: Danish School of Education, Aarhus University.

of the technical courses. An exam from a technical preparatory course gave access to medium level technical courses. The courses were organised as evening classes over two years, making them accessible also for those in work. In 1967, the two-year higher preparatory exam (hf) was introduced as mainly a second chance for adults to prepare for further education. In 1969, a new act on leisure time education was implemented, and the technical preparatory courses became part of the act. This was followed by a change from a vocationally oriented focus preparing for technical courses to a higher degree of general adult education, and the curricula was augmented with subjects from grades 9 and 10 in lower secondary school. It thereby became possible for adults to go back to school to get an exam at lower secondary level at the technical preparatory courses or an exam at upper secondary level at the higher preparatory course. With an act on single subject exam preparing courses for adults from 1977, single subject courses at levels 9 and 10 and higher preparatory courses organised as single subject courses were integrated in the new adult education centres (VUC) (Klinkby, 2004).

The technical preparatory courses, though, were not the only new options for adults who wanted to enter education. In 1960, labour market centres offering vocational education for unskilled workers were established (Klinkby, 2004).

In the 21st century, adult education has gained new attention, and Danes are among those Europeans who participate most in adult education and training (Chisholm, Larson, & Mosseux, 2004; Desjardins, Rubenson, & Milana, 2006, Danish Ministry of Finance, 2006a; Milana, 2008). In addition, there is in the European Union an increased attention on the qualifications of those teaching adults. In the European Commission's action plan on adult learning, "It is always a good time to learn" (*It is always a good time to learn*, 2007), attention is drawn to the important role teachers and trainers play for the quality of the educational programmes. The action plan at the same time concludes that "little attention has been paid to the training (initial and continuing) ... of the adult learning staff" (European Commission, 2007, p. 8).

In the light of this, the paper tries to answer the question: *How are the qualifications of those teaching adults addressed in Danish educational policy (with a special focus on initiatives from the year 2000 till today)?*

Methodology

The results presented in the paper build on an analysis of Danish policy papers from the year 2000 until today. The criterion for the selection of papers has been that they either focus on education of adults or on education and training for adult educators, with a special focus on the last. The selected papers include policy statements and strategies.

The aim of the analysis of policy papers has been to identify policy strategies put forward to enhance the quality in the field of adult education and training. Focus in the analysis, thus, is on the mentioning (or non-mentioning) of qualification of those teaching adults in the Danish strategies for lifelong learning and adult education and training. The analysis deals with adult education receiving some kind of public support only. The huge market of purely private courses is thus not part of the analysis, though they are a major provider of education and training for adults.

Current offers and requirements for those interested in teaching within adult education and training

The market of education and courses for those interested in teaching adults is varied, from very short courses lasting a few weeks to longer education programmes of a couple of years' duration. Further, the entry requirements education programmes and the academic level vary from none to university level.

Among the short courses is the 'Basic course in teaching of adults' (AVG). There are no entry requirements for the course, which is aimed at people with a vocational education interested in teaching adults e.g. within liberal adult education. The course normally has a duration of 120 hours. Having finished the course, it is possible to continue into a 'Further education in teaching of adults' (VOU). The aim of the course is to give an up-to-date introduction to the teaching of adults. The entry requirement for this course is a basic course in teaching of adults or similar qualifications (Milana, 2008). Both the basic and the continued course are thought to be relevant for people interested in teaching in liberal adult education, though there are no required formal competences in the teaching of adults in liberal adult education. If a person is interested in teaching within general or vocational adult education, neither of these two courses meets the requirements.

People interested in teaching within general adult education must either take the education as a teacher in primary and lower secondary school, if interested in teaching at courses corresponding to grades 9 or 10 in compulsory school, or a master degree followed by a professional post graduate teacher training (*Act on general adult education (AVU), Act on higher preparatory exam (hf)*). For those interested in teaching at the labour market programmes or at the technical and mercantile programmes, it is possible to take a post graduate vocational teacher training (Milana, 2008). To be employed as teacher at a technical or mercantile education programme, the teacher training must be finished no later than two years after the person's appointment. For teachers within the labour market programmes, the pedagogical requirements are formal pedagogical competences directed at teaching of adults at a level comparative to what is acquired in post graduate vocational teacher training. Also in this case, the qualification must be acquired no later than two years after the appointment (*Executive order on common descriptions of competences for vocational adult education and training*).

For those interested in qualifications related to adult education at a higher academic level, it is possible to get a one year diploma and/or a two year master in adult education. These courses, however, are not formally required in any of the sectors (general, vocational and liberal adult education). In addition to the courses described above, there are courses directed at teaching within specific areas like people with dyslexia and within Danish as a foreign language that are a requirement for those interested within these areas (Milana, 2008).

Though a range of options exist for those interested in teaching adults, the actual requirements for pedagogic qualification differ between the sectors from no requirements at all within liberal adult education to some requirements within general and vocational adult education. However, even in the cases where a pedagogical qualification is required, it does not always have to be related to the teaching of adults.

Lifelong learning and an interest in adult educators within the Ministry of Education

As mentioned above, the tradition for adult education in Denmark is long. Though the origins of liberal, general and vocationally oriented adult education mix together, the further development of the three strands of adult education has been separated. This has lead to a difference in organisation and financial arrangements, as well as for some years, different governmental affiliations. The boundaries between the three sectors, however, are again being challenged as a result of the shift in political focus from education to learning, and accreditation of prior learning, where it is no longer important where competences have been developed, but instead which competences are present (Milana, 2008). This is also evident from the different strategies related to lifelong learning and adult education and training.

Though lifelong learning is not a new idea, the presidency conclusions from the Lisbon summit in 2000 (*Presidency conclusions. Lisbon European council 23 and 24 March 2000*, 2000) was a kick-start to a new and increased focus on the need for education and training throughout life. At that time, according to a study made by EURYDICE there was already at departmental level in Denmark an understanding of the need for lifelong learning defined as adult education and training. The report further mentioned that lifelong learning in Denmark was aimed at personal development as well as competence development related to the needs of the labour market (Eurydice, 2000).

The same year as the European Council in Lisbon in 2000, the Danish parliament passed an act on vocationally oriented basic and further education for adults, better known as the adult and further education reform (*Act on vocationally oriented basic and further education for adults*, 2000). The aim of the law as stated in the first paragraph was to "provide adults with a chance to improve vocational as well as personal competences through participation in basic and further education" (our translation). The general intention behind the law was, thus, to ease access to adult education and training. The competences of those who would be teaching the adults, however, were neither dealt with in the law nor in the comments to the law. The law was the result of the work in a commission set up in co-operation between the Ministry of Finance, the Ministry of Labour and the Ministry of Education, and led by the Ministry of Finance. In 1999, the commission had published a report on aims and means in publicly financed adult and further education (Danish Ministry of Finance, 1999). In line with the act, the report from the commission did not cover the question of the competences of those teaching the adults.

The lack of attention on competence development for adult educators in the reform, however, did not reflect a general lack of attention.

Also in 2000, the Danish Ministry of Education published the results from a project on quality in the Danish Educational system, 'Quality that can be seen' (Danish Ministry of Education, 2000). According to the ministry, highly qualified teachers is a necessity for a high educational level: "The teachers must master pedagogical methods for communication of subject knowledge and be motivated for teaching and engagement of the students" (our translation) (Danish Ministry of Education, 2000, p. 96). At the same time, it is clear from the mapping of competence development for teachers within adult education and training carried out in relation to the project that this was very sporadic. Neither within general nor liberal adult education were formal pedagogical qualifications a prerequisite for teaching, though there were plans for introduction of such demands in relation to general adult education (Danish Ministry of Education, 2000).

Another project with special focus on teachers within adult education, "Focus on the adult educator", had been launched in 1997. The project was financed by the Ministry of Education. The first report from the project published in 1999 presented a mapping of courses offering pedagogical qualification for adult educators (Danneskiold-Samsøe, 1999). The report pointed at a major increase in the provision of competence development for teachers within adult education, but did not look at actual participation in these courses. The second report from the project was published in 2000, focussing on the need for competence development among the adult educators (Danneskiold-Samsøe & Ingeberg, 2000). The third and last report in the project from 2002 treated qualification of teachers within general adult education (Wahlgren, Danneskiold-Samsøe, Hemmingsen, & Larson, 2002).

In spite of the awareness in the Ministry and among researchers within the field of adult education of the importance of qualifying the teachers within adult education, in the following years, competence development for adult educators continued to be more or less absent in the overall reforms and political strategies for Danish education.

Globalisation – what happened to the interest in the adult educator?

In 2002, two years after the Lisbon meeting, the Danish government launched a plan for economic growth called 'Determined Growth'

(Danish Ministry of Economic and Business Affairs, 2002). Though the plan did not refer to the Lisbon meeting, the aims of the Danish plan was similar to that of the council in Lisbon, and like in Lisbon, one of the means to promote economic growth was education of high quality, including education and training for adults.

As a follow-up in relation to education, the government also in 2002 published an action plan for development of the educational system called 'Better Education'. The plan became the platform for reforms within education in Denmark for the following years. In the plan, the need for high quality education and training as well as high quality of teaching were stressed. Further, related to the actual teaching, the plan highlighted development of pedagogical methods focussing on the individual learner:

> "The teachers must to a greater extent focus on the teaching of the individual pupil and on those skills which the individual pupils should acquire through his or her course of education. This requires a flexible organisation of the work and a chance to use a broad spectrum of pedagogical methods" (Danish Ministry of Education, 2002, p. 80).

How the teachers should acquire the pedagogical methods and competences to teach in this way, however, only caught minor attention in the plan, though a new act on teacher training for teachers in primary and lower secondary school was on the political agenda (Danish National Committee for UNESCO & Danish Ministry of Education, 2004). While "'Job swopping' as well as in-service and further education" (Danish Ministry of Education, 2002, p. 49) in relation to medium-cycle higher education programmes were mentioned in the action plan, high quality teaching at the universities was expected to be a result of increased cooperation between universities and sector research institutions:

> "Strategic alliances and different forms of cooperation between the universities themselves and between universities and sector research institutions can in general be one of the central ways of improving the quality of the teaching" (Danish Ministry of Education, 2002, p. 47).

Education of a high quality in the plan, thus, rather referred to usefulness at the labour market, flexibility, and how well Denmark did in international tests and comparisons than to competence development among the teaching staff. Further, dealing with development of teaching competences the plan only mentioned in-service and further education, while initial education and training for those interested in teaching adults were not touched at all. The plan was followed up in 2004 by a report on how the goals stated in the plan had been met as well as plans for the future (Danish Ministry of Education & Danish Ministry of Science, Technology and Innovation, 2004a). If competence development for teachers within adult education had been almost invisible in the first plan, this was even more the case in the follow-up. In fact only competence development for teachers in primary and lower secondary school was addressed in the report.

In a report from the Danish Presidency for the Nordic Council of Ministers for education, research and ICT also in 2004, it was stated that "In order to ensure the best offers for adults, pedagogical methods and organisation will be stressed as well as an efficient use of the systems for validation of prior learning" (own translation) (Danish Ministry of Education & Danish Ministry of Science, Technology and Innovation, 2004b, p. 4). The report, thus, drew attention to the importance of pedagogy for adult education and training, but once again, nothing was said on how those teaching the adults should acquire the needed competences.

The tripartite committee and a new adult education reform

In September 2004, the Government together with the employers' and employees' organisations (the tripartite committee) set up a committee to map and analyse adult education and training in Denmark, and based on the analysis, make suggestions for Danish adult education and training in the future. In March 2006, the committee presented its work (Danish Ministry of Finance, 2006). The report looked deeper into the supply of and demand for adult education and training among enterprises and individuals. What is most relevant in relation to this paper is the part on the supply of adult education, where one could expect that qualification of the adult educators would have been included in the report. This, however, was not the case. Both the analysis and the resulting suggestions for the future mainly dealt with structural barriers for the use of adult education and training as well as the scale of adult education and training supply and demand.

As a follow-up to the meeting in the tripartite committee, the government and the social partners once again met in September 2006 and October 2007. Like in the 2006-publication from the tripartite committee, qualification of adult educators was not discussed at either of those meetings (Danish Government, 2007, Danish Ministry of Finance, 2006b).

In April 2006, the Danish Government published a strategy for Denmark in the global economy (Danish Government, 2006a). The overall aim of the strategy was to make Denmark one of the most attractive countries in the world to live and work in, a country with strong competitiveness and strong cohesion. To reach these aims, the strategy stressed the need for "world top level education" (Danish Government, 2006a, p. 8). In relation to adult education, the strategy mentioned nine key initiatives: easily accessible and straightforward guidance; easier to get recognition of prior learning; more systematic competence development in companies; more flexible and practice oriented adult education programmes in reading, writing and arithmetic; better language courses for bilingual people; better quality of and more higher education programmes; new model for the special allowance scheme for adult vocational education and training programmes; flexible and differentiated tuition fees and subsidies; and special saving schemes for adult education and continuing training. The initiatives, thus, once again were mainly related to structural and economic factors, while the quality of the adult education and training in form of pedagogic qualification of those teaching the adults was not mentioned.

Nor was qualification of adult educators part of the agreement that the Danish government and three parties from the opposition[14] entered into two months later in June 2006 on initiatives to secure wealth, welfare and investments in the future (Danish Government, 2006b), though one of the themes in the agreement was strengthening of the adult and further education. This is especially striking since the agreements between the government and the three parties from the opposition, following the

---

14 The Social Democrats, The Danish Peoples' Party and the social liberal party ("Det Radikale Venstre").

globalisation strategy and the agreement of wealth, welfare and investments in the future, involved funding of qualification of teachers within vocational education and training in general as well as for teachers within medium range higher education, with a specific focus on those teaching the coming teachers within primary and lower secondary school as well as the coming kindergarten teachers (Danish Government, 2006c; Danish Government, 2006d; Danish Government, 2008).

Also in 2006, the Ministry of Education published a development programme for adult vocational education and training (Danish Ministry of Education, 2006). The aim of the programme was to promote cooperation between vocational education and training institutions and enterprises. And this time, competence development for teachers was mentioned as one out of five key activities: "Organisational and competence development must be implemented at the schools [...] the centres will contribute to development of the needed competences among teachers and educational consultants" (own translation) (Danish Ministry of Education, 2006, p. 7). The ministry, thus, saw a need for development of the teachers' competences if they were to enter into closer cooperation with enterprises.

The present state

In 2007, the Danish Government presented an account of the Danish Strategy for lifelong learning to EU as part of the Lisbon strategy (Danish Ministry of Education, 2007). With reference to both EU's Lisbon Strategy and the Danish government's globalisation strategy, the strategy for lifelong learning presented on the one hand the initiatives already taken in relation to lifelong learning, and on the other hand the planned activities. In relation to adult education and training, the strategy mentioned among the main aims that "There must be relevant, high quality adult education and continuing training for everyone in the labour market which matches the needs and puts particular emphasis on the need for lifelong skills upgrading for those with the lowest level of education" (Danish Ministry of Education, 2007, p. 9). Further, it is stressed in the strategy that "all forms of education and learning should be based on and build on the knowledge, skills and competences of individuals" (p. 9), and it is a public task to provide the relevant education programmes of high quality (Danish Ministry of Education, 2007, p. 21). The quality of adult education and training is, thus, as a focal point in the strategy. In line with most of the other strategies mentioned so far, the strategy, however, does neither define quality nor deal with how qualification of the adult educators can contribute to the quality of the adult education and training.

Though adult education and training has gained much attention in Danish education policy, and some policy papers even stress the need for high quality adult education and training, there is almost complete silence when it comes to the qualification of those who either already teach within adult education and training or would like to do so.

Conclusion

The aim of the paper was to analyse Danish adult education policy from 2000 till today, with a specific focus on qualification of adult educators. From the mapping of the current offers and requirements for those interested in teaching adults, it is clear that requirements for pedagogical qualifications with a focus on teaching of adults is not the rule, but rather an exception. Except for the labour market education programmes (AMU), a special focus on teaching of adults is not mentioned in relation to the pedagogical requirements within neither vocational nor general adult education. Qualifications in teaching children and young people are thus considered to be enough. Within liberal adult education, no qualifications are required at all. Further, neither for vocational adult education nor higher preparatory exam courses is initial pedagogical education and training of the teachers required. While teachers within higher preparatory exam courses are expected to acquire the pedagogical education and training within one year after employment, teachers within vocational education and training can wait till two year after their employment to get the qualifications.

This lack of acknowledgement of a need for qualification of those teaching adults is also seen in most of the Danish policy and strategies related to adult education since the year 2000. In spite of some focus on the quality of adult education and training, qualification of those expected to deliver this quality is almost absent in the papers and strategies. To answer the question posed in the beginning of the paper: The qualifications of those teaching adults are only sporadically addressed in Danish educational policy from year 2000 till today.

References

Act on general adult education (AVU), lov nr 311 af 30/04/2008.
Act on higher preparatory exam (hf), lov nr 445 af 08/05/2007.
Act on vocationally oriented basic and further education for adults, lov nr. 488 af 31/05/2000.
Chisholm, L., Larson, A., & Mosseux, A.-F. (2004). *Lifelong learning: Citizens' views in close-up. Findings from a dedicated Eurobarometer survey.* Luxembourg: Office for Official Publications of the European Communities.
Danish Ministry of Economic and Business Affairs (2002). *Vækst med vilje.* Copenhagen.
Danish Ministry of Education (2000). *Kvalitet der kan ses.* Copenhagen.
Danish Ministry of Education (2002). *Better Education - action plan.* Copenhagen.
Danish Ministry of Education (2006). *Voksen- og efteruddannelse i centrum - et udviklingsprogram for kompetencecentre på erhvervsskoler, AMU-centre og social- og sundhedsskoler.* Copenhagen.
Danish Ministry of Education (2007) *Denmark's strategy for lifelong learning. education and lifelong skills upgrading for all.* Copenhagen.
Danish Ministry of Education & Danish Ministry of Science, Technology and Innovation (2004a). *Bedre uddannelser - fra ord til handling - status tre år efter regeringens tiltrædelse.* Copenhagen.
Danish Ministry of Education & Danish Ministry of Science, Technology and Innovation (2004b). *Globaliseringens udfordring til faglighed og kvalitet inden for uddannelse, forskning og IT.* Copenhagen.
Danish Ministry of Finance (1999). *Mål og midler i offentligt finansieret voksen- og efteruddannelse.* Copenhagen.
Danish Ministry of Finance (2006a). *Livslang opkvalificering og uddannelse for alle på arbejdsmarkedet - rapport fra trepartsudvalget - bind 1: Den fremtidige voksen- og efteruddannelsesindsats.* Copenhagen.
Danish Ministry of Finance (2006b). *Styrket voksen- og efteruddannelsesindsats er et fælles ansvar.* Copenhagen.
The Danish National Commission for UNESCO & Danish Ministry of Education (2004). *National report on the development of education in Denmark since 2001. 47th international conference on education. Geneva, 8.-11. September 2004.* Copenhagen.
Danish Government (2006a). *Progress, innovation and cohesion. Strategy for Denmark in the global economy - summary.* Copenhagen.
Danish Government (2006b). *Velfærdsaftalen (aftale mellem regeringen (Venstre*

og Det Konservative Folkeparti) og Socialdemokraterne, Dansk Folkeparti og Det Radikale Venstre om initiativer til sikring af fremtidens velstand og velfærd og investeringer i fremtiden). Copenhagen.

Danish Government (2006c) *Opfølgning på velfærdsaftalen*. Copenhagen.

Danish Government (2006d). *Aftale om udmøntning af globaliseringsaftalen*. Copenhagen.

Danish Government (2007). *Markant styrkelse af erhvervsrettet voksen- og efteruddannelse*. Copenhagen.

Danish Government (2008). *Opfølgning på gobaliseringsaftalerne. Aftale mellem regeringen (Vestre og Konservative), Socialdemokraterne, Dansk Folkeparti og Det Radikale Venstre.* (2008). Copenhagen.

Danneskiold-Samsøe, S. (1999). *Kortlægning af almenpædagogiske lærerkvalificeringsforløb*. Copenhagen: Danish Ministry of Education & The Research Centre for Adult Education.

Danneskiold-Samsøe, S., & Ingeberg, T. (2000). *Behovet for lærerkvalificering*. Copenhagen: Danish Ministry of Education.

Desjardins, R., Rubenson, K., & Milana, M. (2006). *Unequal chances to participate in adult learning: International perspectives.* Paris: UNESCO IIEP.

Eurodice (2000). *Lifelong learning: The contribution of education systems in the member states of the European Union. Results of the Eurydice survey*. Brussels.

European Commission (2007). *Action plan on adult learning. It is always a good time to learn.* (2007). Brussels.

Executive order on common descriptions of competences for vocational adult education and training, bekendtgørelse nr 802 af 22/09/2003.

Klinkby, E. (2004). *Historien om VUC - fra teknisk forberedelse til livslang læring.* Frederiksberg: Roskilde Universitetsforlag.

Korsgaard, O. (1997). *Kampen om lyset. Dansk voksenoplysning gennem 500 år.* Copenhagen: Gyldendal.

Milana, M. (2008). *Initial education and training pathways for Danish adult educators.* Paper presented at the ASEM conference, Beijing, China.

Presidency conclusions. Lisbon European Council 23 and 24 March 2000. (2000). Lisbon: Commission of European Communities.

Wahlgren, B., Danneskiold-Samsøe, S., Hemmingsen, L., & Larson, A. (2002). *Fokus på voksenlæreren. Om kvalificering af lærere inden for den almene voksenundervisning.* Copenhagen: Danish Ministry of Education.

Quality for Adult Educators?
A Swedish outlook

Petros Gougoulakis

Introduction

Europe as a whole is undergoing a major transformation, due to global competition, affecting all societal sectors. In March 2000, the European Council affirmed that Europe moved into the Knowledge Age, implying extensive changes for cultural, economic and social life.[15] Education and lifelong learning is perceived to lie at the heart of the transformation towards a knowledge-based economy and society.

Lifelong learning has without exception become the prevailing educational ideology of our post-industrial time functioning as the guiding principle for provision and participation across the full continuum of learning contexts for all EU citizens. Thus, not only youth education of good quality has to be guaranteed but adults must also have access to educational opportunities to constantly renew their skills or develop new ones to handle the challenges of today, and actively participate in the shaping of Europe's future. According to policy making rhetoric the future challenges for the European Union is to create a joint labour market by enabling well educated and trained citizens to take their qualifications across borders.[16]

Fruitful lifelong learning opportunities in the diverse field of adult education need to be supported by well qualified educators. Educators' role and status are also dependent on how well they are qualified for their task and the recognition they obtain. Quality and professional development – professionalization - of adult educators are core issues of

---

15 Commission of the European Communities (2000). *A Memorandum on Lifelong Learning*.
16 European Commission. *Education & Training* (http://ec.europa.eu/education/index_en.htm) Last update: 14 May 2009

current research run by the European Research Group on Competencies in the Field of Adult and Continuing Education which was set up by the German Institute of Adult Education (DIE). (Ekkehard & Lattke 2008)

In 2007 the DIE Group initiated the European Conference "*Qualifying the Actors in Adult and Continuing Education* (Q-ACT)". One of the aims of the conference was "to review the state of the art in Europe, share experience and good practice", which resulted in a survey with the same title. Based on empirical research carried out by a Delphi-Method, the survey started up in 2008 in several European countries.[17] Among other outcomes, the project is expected to

a. identify a profile of core competencies for educators/teachers in Adult and Continuing Education
b. create knowledge which may support the introduction and establishment of measures for the education and qualification of adult educators,
c. raise the professional abilities of adult educators and
d. specify the meaning of "professionalization" in the adult education field.

Since 2008, measures are taken throughout Europe to introduce various schemes for increasing transparency on qualification levels in terms of learning outcomes – what a learner knows, understands and is able to do – in order to link them to the European Qualifications Framework for lifelong learning (EQF) (European Communities, 2008).[18] EQF is

---

17 From October 2009 the study is carried out in the shape of the EU-funded project "QF2TEACH - Qualified to Teach" in which 7 countries are involved, namely Germany, Sweden, Holland, Switzerland, Italy, Romania, and Poland. Every national partner is responsible for the survey in respective country. (German Institute for Adult Education, 2009. *Qualified to Teach*)
In the Delphi-Method research design, experts in the participating countries will be asked in several waves to analyse data collected both with standardised as well as with open questions, using both quantitative and qualitative procedures. The collective elaboration of the empirical data in the Delphi-procedure is aiming to facilitate the compilation of future-oriented core competences, striving towards a consensus among the experts in the involved countries. (Linstone & Turoff eds., 2002. The *Delphi Method. Techniques and Applications.*)
18 The EQF is an EU-wide tool which links countries' qualifications systems to-

an initiative to create a translating facility for referencing academic degrees and other learning qualifications among EU member states. When the decision on EQF is taken, all countries participating in the process will pursue with national decisions on how to adapt the national qualifications systems to the overarching European framework. Traditionally, qualifications are mostly described in terms of input such as length of study or type of institution attended. The EQF, on the contrary, emphasises the results of learning, in terms of knowledge, skills and competences, rather than focusing on inputs such as length of study.

The idea of learning outcomes instead of the traditional view is also reflected in the German proposal in following normative manner: "it is important what people are able to do and not where they have learned it."[19] Obviously, the way EQF considers qualifications aims to capture the entire width of theoretical, practical and social skills that is regarded of great relevance to fulfil another overall objective, namely that of achieving and maintaining employability. The qualification framework is, at the same time, a concrete recognition of the fact that Europe's education and training systems are so diverse. The EQF shift to learning outcomes marks a willingness to facilitate comparison and cooperation between countries and institutions. The question needed to be asked is whether the recommended eight reference levels (See annex II in EQF, European Communities, 2008) really confine an individual's full capacity and not just what can be measured within the particular frame of reference.

Ta panta rei

Heraclitus' statement *Ta Panta Rei* ("Everything Floats") could be regarded as a suitable description of our time's all-encompassing changes. Everything is changing and does so at a rapid pace. The way we understand learning, where and how it takes place, and for what kinds of purposes, is subjected to comprehensive reviews. Teaching and learning methods are

---

gether, acting as a translation device to make qualifications more readable and comparable across Europe. The EQF has two principal aims: to promote citizens' mobility between countries and to facilitate their lifelong learning. (European Communities, 2008. *The European Qualifications Framework for Lifelong Learning (EQF)*.

19 http://ec.europa.eu/education/news/news1245_en.htm

expected to adapt to various interests, needs and demands of individuals and groups in our highly culturally and ethnically diverse societies. Not least, educators' skills need to be raised, adapted and developed if they are to be in line with *the state of the art* pedagogical thinking. Furthermore, adult educators are identified as one of the key target groups in the Commission Communication on Adult Learning, which urge Member States to put in place initial and continuing professional measures to qualify and up-skill the adult-learning staff in Europe. (Ekkehard & Lattke 2008)

Knowledge, skills and aptitudes are considered to be a major factor in the EU's innovation, productivity and competitiveness of the European workforce. The process of globalization, the rapid pace of change, and the continuous roll-out of new technologies call for every citizen of Europe not only to keep their specific job-related skills up-to-date, but also possess some generic competences that will enable them to adapt to change. Apparently, there is a need for new skills and competences for mastering the new digital world. Furthermore, there is a need to gain a deeper understanding of the opportunities, challenges and even ethical questions posed by new technologies.

This kind of reasoning about the role of education is significant for today's education policy rhetoric at a European level. It can best be illustrated by the case of the European Framework for Key Competences for Lifelong Learning, adopted by the Council and the European Parliament, at the end of 2006. The aim of this framework is to identify and define the key competences that citizens require for their personal fulfilment, social inclusion, active citizenship and employability in our knowledge-based society.

> *In this climate of rapid change, there is increasing concern about our social cohesion. There is a risk that many Europeans feel left behind and marginalised by globalisation and the digital revolution. The resulting threat of alienation implies a need to nurture democratic citizenship; it requires people to be informed and concerned about their society and active in it. The knowledge, skills and aptitudes that everyone needs must change as a result.*[20]

---

[20] Recommendation of the European Parliament and of the Council of 18 December 2006 on key competences for lifelong learning. Official Journal of the European Union L394. (http://eur-lex.europa.eu/LexUriServ/site/en/oj/2006/l_394/l_39420061230en00100018.pdf)

In what follows, I will introduce some concepts frequently used in the current education policy discourse, which inevitably may initiate changes in the content and infrastructure of national education systems.

Competences as "learning outcome"

The concept of competence has in recent years instigated its intrusion into the regular educational vocabulary.

According to a widespread definition, learning means *"relatively sustainable changes in an individual's competence as a result by the individual's interaction with the environment."* (Ellström 1996, p. 147, my translation). Classical learning psychology perceives learning as *"the change of inner and outer behaviour"*. The scope is widened in modern cognitive psychology which identifies learning with *"changes of the individual's conceptions, knowledge (mental models) or intellectual skills."* Ellström goes further and connects learning to individual action and competence. The substance of learning then becomes a change in the individual competence which he defines as *"an individual's potential capacity to act in relation to a certain task, situation and context, namely the ability to successfully (according to their own or others' criteria) perform a piece of work, including ability to identify, exploit and, if possible, extend the space of interpretation, action and set of values that the work allows."* (Ellström 1992, p. 21, my translation)

Competence as a concept and its more powerful form, *key competence*, has its roots in the information technology explosion of the 1970's that raised issues regarding what basic knowledge and skills people need in order to meet and to cope with the challenges of a rapidly changing society. At the same time, key skills are also understood as being "keys" necessary for opening more specific skills. There are many attempts to define and determine the concept of competence.[21]

---

21 According to a source referenced by Sven-Eric Liedman (2008, *Nycklar till ett framgångsrikt liv? – Om EU:s nyckelkompetenser*, footnote 8) there are approximately 2000 definitions of competence, namely: Yvonne-Marie Ruedin, "Les clés pour l'emploi et l'arbre des compétences", Panorama nr 6/2002, s. 19 (http://www.panorama.ch/pdf/2002/Heft_6_2002/pan2619.pdf).
The difference between competence and skill is discussed by Tiana (2004) in an article about how to develop key competencies in education:
"From a strictly conceptual viewpoint, competence has a broader meaning than skill and many analysts consider a competence to include several skills. If we ac-

Apparently, the concept of competence is loaded with different meanings depending on the perspective from which it is approached. For example, philosophers are interested in capturing the timeless human competencies and address key competencies that are generally independent of culture, context and personal characteristics. For sociologists, competencies imply empowerment of individuals and groups to preserve their autonomy and exercise their rights without infringing on that of others, and to cope in and across various social fields. The economists, finally, calculate the value of skills in the workplace and labour market and usually talk about competencies that the working force need in order *"to increase productivity and succeed in the labor market, with success defined in the 'maximization of income' and 'return to education' in financial terms"*. They also put emphasis on knowledge and skills which result in increased competitiveness in the market. (Zhou Nan-Zhao, p. 5)[22]

From an interdisciplinary view the notion of competence is perceived enclosing the external requirements, e.g., from the labour market, as well as the individual's own abilities in terms of knowledge and skills of cognitive, practical and social character along with ethical principles, emotions and attitudes. Ultimately, the notion of competence is used to signify an individual's ability to carry out an activity and/or to deal with challenges and complex demands in a successful way. However, such an "out-turned" ability's functionality[23] is dependent on the support of other "inward" mental abilities, capacities and dispositions. (Rychen and Tiana 2004; Ellström 1992)

"Key competence" is another term that nowadays is used frequently in various policy documents. If **competence** is defined as a combination of knowledge, skills, attitudes and mental abilities appropriate to a particular situation for *"necessary for everyone"*, **key competences** are *"those that support personal fulfilment, social inclusion, active citizenship and employ-*

---

cept that distinction, then the concept of competence should be considered as broader, more general and a higher level of cognition and complexity than the concept skill." (p.73)

22 Zhou Nan-Zhao: *Four 'Pillars of Learning' for the Reorientation and Reorganization of Curriculum: Reflections and Discussions.*

23 "the quality or state of being functional; *especially:* the particular set of functions or capabilities associated with computer software or hardware or an electronic device" (http://www.merriam-webster.com/dictionary/FUNCTIONALITY)

ment" (OECD 2005; Commission of the European Communities 2005). It is, thus, unclear in what sense key competences are "keys". A feasible interpretation might be that the key competences "open" the way for more specific, including occupation-specific, skills. (Liedman 2008).

Although the concept *competence/key competence* has multitudinous usages, *skills* refer to a given ability and, ultimately, to a contingency and a disposition, required when performing a certain task which is based on specific knowledge. Proctor and Dutta (1995, p. 18) define skill as "*goal-directed, well-organized behavior that is acquired through practice and performed with economy of effort*" (Winterton, Delamare - Le Deist & Stringfellow 2005, p. 12)

Professionalisation and professionalism

The concept profession is used differently, like many others within the social sciences, depending on from what perspective it is approached. It is important, however, to make a distinction between professionalisation and professionalism which are sometimes used as synonyms. Professionalization refers to the aspirations for social position and status of a professional group, while professionalism focuses on the internal quality of a profession. Professionalism is dealing with the qualities and acquired skills of professionals - actual competences - necessary to successfully exercise the profession. Englund (2007, p. 143) goes a step further and proposes the use of the concept *didactic competence*, in order to avoid confusion which the use of the terms professionalization and professionalism might cause. According to Ekholm (2007, p. 143), the professional level of a profession is determined by factors dealing with

a. the specific knowledge base of the profession
b. the responsibility for the development of the profession,
c. the existence of professional ethics
d. the control of who may exercise the profession and
e. the degree of professional autonomy

Certainly, Ekholm's reasoning refers to how the professionalism of primary and secondary school teachers is perceived in relation to the above criteria, but it can also be used to treat adult educators as a professional group. The traditional use of the concept of teachers' professionalization has stressed the proficiency of teaching a subject. Teachers have had the task of disseminating knowledge but there are very few teachers who are specialists in their fields of knowledge. Teachers' professional knowledge thus has a wide and generic direction, not least because they face groups of students with different needs and conditions. At the same time teaching requires specific knowledge, e.g. on how learning takes place in relation to learners' developmental needs, on how the educational materials should be structured and processed in order to promote learning and, additionally, knowledge of human behaviour in group contexts. This approach of the teaching profession has emphasized the didactical aspects of teaching, taking teachers' subject knowledge for granted. Regarding the responsibility and initiative for the development of professional content and direction, as well as control over who gets access to the profession, teachers as a collective seem to have very little influence. This is also true in the case of the profession's ethics since teachers, as professional collectives, have no control and sanction mechanisms or legal obligation concerning observance and compliance of the ethical principles. On the contrary, the degree of professional autonomy, in the sense that no other than the teacher determines how to think and act in a teaching situation, seems to be relatively high. Due to this circumstance teachers are often considered as professionals. (Ekholm)

Development of professional teaching competencies is mainly linked to the formal teacher training. A modern professional education at an academic level is arranged on the basis of knowledge that it is believed future teachers need to master to facilitate others' learning. At the same time it is expected that this knowledge will create a foundation for continuing learning (Docherry 1996; Folkesson 2005, p. 67). The skilled teacher is, therefore, expected to take a professional responsibility for his or her own continuing learning process which is supposed to be mostly of informal character. It is informal because it is not institutionalized or prestructured in a set curricula and model in order to achieve the predefined knowledge. However, this does not mean that informal learning takes place only unconsciously and unintentionally. Informal learning is also a highly purposeful and autonomous activity. (Cross 2007, Deer Richardson & Wolfe 2001, Bron-Wojciechowska 1996).

How teachers relate to their own professional (competence) development has been the subject of the so-called *Teachers thinking research movement* that focuses on teachers' thinking about their own experience from practice (Larsson 2006; Goodson 2005; Carlgren; Kelchtermans 1993;

Schön 1983). Teachers' professional development is a lifelong process during which the individual skills go hand-in-hand with the overall school development (Fullan & Hargreaves 1992).

Teachers' professional core consists of potential competencies whose development gradually takes place during the course of their professional life. Such a development model has been presented by Kugel (1993) who has studied the university teachers' professional development. Kugel's model indicates that teachers initially focus on mastering their role in the classroom (Stage I: competencies of the **self**). When this has been successfully completed they focus their attention on how to understand and organize their subject in order to convey it (Stage II: The competences of the instruction **subject**). After that the teachers feel familiar with their own educational role and confident enough with the subject; they can pay attention to students' abilities and learning needs (Stage III: **student**-centered didactic competences).

Although the model gives the impression that the phases of development follow a certain order, it is far from certain that is always the case. However, it is reasonable to assume that the usual pattern is as Kugel proposes it. Fundamental in this case is that the model captures the qualitative leap that occurs during the changeover to the third step. What such a model emphasizes is the restructuring of teacher competencies signifying a perspective alteration, from their own instruction to student learning.

Ultimately, the model describes a teacher's professional evolution by which a basic ability appears to be managing the relationship between the three competence dimensions of teaching. Mastering the relationship between self, subject and student creates conditions and space for teachers to act, as well as freedom to choose among a large repertoire of teaching strategies depending on the educational situation in question. Professional experience and the ability to reflect on one's own professional practice is of great importance.

The cited model could be used as a structuring and classified principle of adult educators' generic competencies. The different stages of an educator's professional development may constitute a coherent and sound, although broad, set of key competencies related to the different skills that teachers need to acquire in order to fulfil their tasks ("mission"?).

Adult educators' key competencies could be placed under Kugel's stages which can be perceived as three broad dimensions of an educator's competence profile. Instead of a long list of key competences related to specific subject domains should this profile embrace sets of competences integrated across learning domains.

Another set of competence categories is listed within the previously mentioned Q-ACT Project, namely:
1. personal competencies
2. social competencies
3. didactical competencies
4. methodological competencies
5. societal and institutional competencies (Nuissl & Lattke 2008, p. 54-55)

The DeSeCo Project introduces yet another conceptual framework for key competencies classifying them into three broad categories:

> *First, individuals need to be able to use a wide range of tools for interacting effectively with the environment: both physical ones such as information technology and socio-cultural ones such as the use of language. They need to understand such tools well enough to adapt them for their own purposes – to use tools interactively.*
>
> *Second, in an increasingly interdependent world, individuals need to be able to engage with others, and since they will encounter people from a range of backgrounds, it is important that they are able to interact in heterogeneous groups.*
>
> *Third, individuals need to be able to take responsibility for managing their own lives, situate their lives in the broader social context and act autonomously.*[24]

Based on the work of the DeSeCo project, Tiana (2004) makes a tentative proposal for key competencies for education systems dividing them in two main groups, namely
a) **curriculum-bounded competencies**, such as ability to communicate with other, basic science/math skills, computer literacy and media competence
b) **cross-curricular competencies**, which include metacognitive competencies, intra-personal competencies, interpersonal competencies,

---

24 OECD: *Definition and Selection of Key Competencies* (DeSeCo): *Executive Summary*. (p. 5) http://www.oecd.org/dataoecd/47/61/35070367.pdf

and positional competencies (coping with complexity and dealing with diversity/change).

Hoskins & Fredriksson (2008) line up Tianas proposal in the following Table 1:

Table 1: Key competencies for education systems: a tentative proposal
Source: (Tiana, 2004 p. 51)

Curriculum- bound competencies	Cross-curriculum competencies
Ability to communicate with others, both orally and in writing: – oral and written mastery of the mother tongue – reading comprehension – mastery of at least one foreign language	Metacognitive competencies – problem solving – developing learning strategies – critical judgement – divergent thinking
Basic mathematics skills and numeracy	Intrapersonal competencies – management of motivation and emotions – self-concept – developing personal autonomy
Computer literacy and media competence	Interpersonal competencies – capacity of joining and functioning democratically in groups – ability to relate well to other people – ability to play by the rules and to manage and resolve conflicts
Capacity of situating in the world of the individual – knowledge of the natural and social world – development of civic attitudes	Positional competencies – ability for coping with complexity – dealing with diversity and change

The competencies mentioned above do evidently not specifically refer to educators but are competencies which all individuals are expected to cultivate because of the widely accepted notion that a well-educated, knowledgeable, highly qualified citizenry is seen as playing an eminent role in facing the challenges of the present and the future. The development of these competencies is linked to notions of lifelong learning for every citizen and to notions of how adult learning should be organised and carried out. Not least, the kind of knowledge, skills, and competencies which are important to individuals and to society as a whole affect the adult educators' professional competencies, knowledge and skills. But who is the adult educator and what kind of competencies is he/she in need of?

The adult educator

The notion "adult educator" indicates a broad range of individuals with the common characterization "one who helps adults learn". If the description is appropriate then the group *adult educators* should include
a. professional adult educators who have been prepared specifically for this vocation, particularly within formal educational institutions
b. group leaders in non-formal education including voluntary associations
c. training officers and staff administrators in corporations.

Except the first category above, adult educators have little or no formal instruction preparing them for the assignment to "help adults learn". (Henschke 1998)

Here "formal" means a teacher programme regulated in the Law, which gives access to a profession that requires qualifications based on formal studies. This doesn't mean that adult educators without formal adult teacher training lack qualifications and skills needed to help adults learn. They may well have acquired them either through self-directed studies or participation in various specially designed courses for adult educators.

Below, I will present two major groups of Swedish adult educators and how they prepare for their professional task: study circle leaders in popular education and teachers in the formal adult education sector.

Study Circle Leaders

The training offered to study circle leaders by the Swedish Popular Adult Education Associations ("Studieförbund")[25] is the only and almost obligatory preparation for the task of "teaching" adults in study circles.[26] Circle Leadership training is an internal matter for each Studieförbund and adapted to its respective pedagogical vision and learning activity profile. It is therefore based on specific ideas of what it means to educate adults and an equally determined view of the human being and learning as well as the importance of education for individual fulfilment. Since Popular Education ("Folkbildning") is largely financed with public funds, the State also expects some results as a legitimizing basis for its support, such as strengthening democracy and civic virtues, compensating educational disparities, and broadening people's interest and participation in culture. Beside political motives of equality and justice, the State also raises a range of "developing areas" of great relevance for popular adult education. Through studies and cultural activities, adults are given opportunities to become responsible individuals and citizens. The idea of *bildning* ("Bildung") unites and permeates everything from studies in study circles to cultural activities, implemented by the popular education organizations together with their partners. It implies an obligation to use

---

25 *Studieförbund* are nation-wide non-formal study organizations for adults. Today there are nine study associations which are supported by the State. Each study association has a more or less marked profile depending on which popular movements/organizations are members in the association.

26 The study circle "studiecirkeln" is the most common form of learning activity in Popular Adult Study Associations. In the study circles participants learn different subjects in accordance to their learning needs and wishes. Every year about 310 000 circles are organized all over the country with a total of 2.5 million participants. (Since many people participate in more than one circle per year the real number of participants is estimated to between one and a half million and two million.).

The official view of popular education in the most recent Act of 1997 maintains that

"(p)opular education is and should be free and voluntary. This free and voluntary popular educational work enables all to seek knowledge on the basis of their own experience, preferences and learning style, without limitation from demands for results, and without mechanisms of exclusion. The approach permits dialogue, involvement and questioning, without a preconceived framework. By reason of this, popular education fulfils a role not covered by any other educational institution, a role which also contributes to maintaining the vitality of democracy." (Regeringens proposition 1997/98:115, p. 5 – my translation)

the aid for the development of the participants' abilities in accordance with their needs. (Borgström, Gougoulakis & Höghielm 1998; Gougoulakis 2001, 2006; Gougoulakis & Bogataj 2007)

Popular Adult Education's view of *bildning* and knowledge embraces all people. Historically, the Swedish popular education had a special status in the educational system and acted as an alternative that also affected the pedagogical thinking in the formal education sector. Its features are explained if we consider the special relationship between the autonomous popular education movement and the democratic social movements – some of the latter could be regarded as protest movements. Education was for the social movements a struggling tool for better living conditions, a more equal and humane society.

Popular adult education organizations' pedagogical and ideological profile is presented in pamphlets and target documents, and hopefully forms the basis of not only the content of the training of the circle leaders but also the actual learning process in study circles. Characteristics of a learning process, according to popular education pedagogical tradition, are the high influence of student participants, the experience-based learning, the social interaction between the participants and the deliberative and reflective conversation. Learning in the study circles should ideally be cooperative.

Popular education activities are not driven by curricula, syllabi or marking scales but are nevertheless systematic. Regularity implies that the participants and the study circle leader, approved by the popular adult education association, will come to an agreement on a structure, which includes learning outcomes, content, learning material and learning activities over a set period of time. A great pedagogical responsibility lies on circle leaders to create and maintain the interest of the participants to study the subject and motivate them to go into a collective learning process. This learning process is free but not arbitrary. Its character is shaped by the participants and the leader's intentions with learning.

Who the circle leader is, what competencies are expected from a circle leader and why someone chooses to become a circle leader, is an almost unexplored field of research. This may seem remarkable considering the fact that popular education has a long tradition in Sweden. Popular adult education activities, as part of the country's adult education infrastructure, need to be further explored concerning the adult learners' study conditions and the quality improvement of the "adult-related" learning. Regarded as "professionals", circle leaders, as well as other adult educators, are expected to imply a pedagogy that takes into account adults' expectations, assumptions, experiences and living conditions in the circle work (Andersson, E. 2001; 2006; Gougoulakis 2001; 2006). Evidently, it is impossible to equate the non-formal popular adult education with other formal adult education, but similarities may occur as the former compete, in some respects, with e.g. municipal adult education ("Komvux") in terms of courses offered and target groups. Against this background and in a situation where popular adult education is in search of a new identity in today's relatively vaguely outlined adult education landscape, more knowledge is needed on the characteristics of circle leadership. In addition to the research already carried out during the 1990s and 2000s (SOU 1996:159; SOU 2000:28; Andersson, P. 2006; SOU 2004:30) there is need for further research with focus on methodological aspects on learning-teaching processes relating to the circle leadership, and on different features of the multifaceted learning process in study circles, e.g. the nature and the effect of popular adult learning on civic virtues, on "civic disciplinary", democratic fostering and power relations in society (compare Larsson 2006).

The distinctive pedagogical character of popular adult education and the renewal of its contents and working methods can, after all, be maintained by the dedicated efforts of its staff. For the study associations, the qualification and skill development of their circle leaders is a key factor for the enhancement and assurance of the quality of learning (see Regeringens proposition 2005/06:192, p. 60-62).

Adult Educators in the formal adult education

Adult Education in Sweden is wide-ranging and offered at different levels by a variety of operators. The adult educational landscape is undergoing major changes, both organizational and pedagogical-didactic. An increased demand for adult teaching and training skills proves to be the result of changing views about the importance of learning for the individuals and the evolution of working life as well. Nowadays, an adult educator is currently involved in many tasks which requires a unique ability to cope with learning situations with adult participants, like, for instance, analyzing educational needs, planning and managing the training needs of adult participants of different ages and in different environments, and developing studying methods tailored to adult learners' individual living conditions. This is particularly important to take into account in the growing number of vocational training programmes for adults - an area expected to expand further.

Thus, the framing of the adult education area is distinguished and looks different from that in schools for adolescents. The formal adult education is characterized by great flexibility as a result of the attention it must pay to adult participants' life experiences, not least their experiences from working life. The government bill for the current teacher education (Regeringens proposition 1999/2000:135, p. 23) states:

> *The Committee proposes that for those students who intend to teach adults, there must be specific specialties relating to the education of adults. The Government agrees with the Committee's proposal assuming that training of this kind will be organized. The government also believes, like the Committee, that pedagogy of adults should be included in the general pedagogical subject area.* (my translation)

The bill also states that the new (year 2000) teacher training will help teachers to teach in different kinds of schools and postulates that during their training prospective teachers will acquire relevant knowledge on adult learning.

However, the results of a survey, conducted by The National Centre for Lifelong Learning (www.encell.se) in the autumn of 2003, showed that there was no teacher training institute, of those who answered the survey, which offered students a specialization in the field of adult education. Even within the general education course this topic appeared to be limited.

Encell's mapping was verified later by an evaluation of the new teacher-training programmes and the follow-up of the reform in teacher training conducted by the National Agency for Higher Education in 2004 (HSV 2005:17 R). According to the evaluation none of the teacher education institutes in the country even designed a specialization with focus on adult education and learning. Apparently, adult teacher training is marginalized in comparison to primary and secondary teachers' training. The HSV's evaluation (Part 1, p. 126) pointed out that not only is this subject area "in backwater", but preparation for teaching adults also seems to be "an almost forgotten" story (ibid., p. 168).

The current Inquiry HUT07 (SOU 2008:109) on a new teacher education programme is also addressing adult education. It states that the training of adults embraces several educational settings with different needs of teaching skills. It notes that the largest volume of adult education takes place within enterprises and government agencies and that it is common for teachers to go into service in this large area, but hitherto there are no formal teacher training requirements to be employed as an educator. The study also notes that adult education in general is "a large market" for teacher-trained people, and believes there is every reason for teacher training institutions to point out these possibilities for teachers-to-be as well as for employers in search of qualified educators. The Inquiry proposes a teacher education programme, with a common core of educational science, aiming to give future teachers a thorough foundation on which they can build during their career by continuous development of their professional skills that also should be useful outside the compulsory school system (p. 285-290).

Today's formal adult education is guided by the Curriculum for the non-compulsory school system (Lpf 94). According to that, "adult education in municipal adult education and the national state schools for adults (SSV) shall, taking account of the pupils' earlier education and experience, deepen and develop the pupils' knowledge as a basis for working life and further studies as well as for participation in civic life" (Lpf 94, p. 8). Knowledge goals are the same for both young persons and adults, but course contents, duration and emphasis do not need to be identical. (ibid., p. 9)

As for the teachers in adult education the Curriculum provides, inter alia, that they shall

- *take as the starting point each individual pupil's needs, preconditions, experience and thinking,*
- *reinforce the pupils' self-confidence as well as their willingness and ability to learn,*
- *make clear the values and perspectives that knowledge is based on and encourage pupils to take a position on how their knowledge can be used,*
- *co-operate with other teachers in the work of achieving the goals of education,*
- *use in the education the knowledge and experience of social and working life which the pupils have or acquire during their education,*
- *take account of developments in pedagogical research and relevant subject areas, and apply these in the education programme.* (p. 13)

Curricula for the compulsory (Lpo 94) and the non-compulsory school system (Lpf 94) have a similar structure regarding the values, objectives and tasks. A comparison between the two shows a remarkable difference in the perceptions of students' learning. Lpo 94 states that schooling shall *"promote learning in which the individual is stimulated to acquire knowledge"*, while Lpf 94 focuses on *"disseminating information"*. Given the fact that there is an established andragogic "truth", that adult learners are likely to be more mature and motivated to acquire knowledge (e.g. Knowles 1990), it is remarkable that the author could formulate the task of adult education in the curriculum in such an obviously uninformed manner.

It should be stressed that the Inquiry HUT07 in its review of the various forms of adult education concludes that these are too different to allow a specific teacher training for adult education. At the same time it considers that the various proposed teacher specialisations cover the need of educators for adult learning settings. Regarding the formal adult education and its tasks the Inquiry comes to the conclusion that *"in principle, special teaching competence is not needed for municipal adult education in addition to relevant teacher specializations in different subjects, although it is advantageous if an adult educational approach could permeate the core courses (in teacher training programmes). For basic adult education even primary school teachers can be considered as far as basic language and math development is concerned."* (SOU 2008:109, p. 287 – my translation)

Despite the emphasis on how large the adult education labour market is, the Inquiry also highlights the need for more research concerning the field of adult education, as well as opportunities for academic institutions, where such research is already undertaken, to add an adult learning profile to their teacher training. (ibid., p. 290)

Skills requirements/competencies for educators

Let us take a glance on how the Inquiry HUT07 (SOU 2008:109) addresses the issue of competencies for a *"Sustainable teacher education"*.

The Inquiry analyses the skills requirements for all categories of teachers and with respect to their essence divides them into three levels:

Level I consists of an **overall dimension** composed of four perspectives meant to set their stamp on all teacher education. These are

- a scientific and critical approach,
- a historical perspective,
- an international dimension, and
- an ICT-perspective meant to function as a pedagogic resource.

The scientific and critical approach is intended to foster future teachers' normative attitudes so as to make them "*aware of and able to evaluate different educational methods and theories*". The historical and international perspectives broaden the students' knowledge in time and space to counteracting a narrowly contemporary and national view of school and learning. The last perspective is regarded as an educational resource and "*an absolutely essential part of a teacher education programme*" in today's digitalized society.

Level II encompasses, according the Inquiry's opinion, a certain set of knowledge and skills that all teachers need, regardless of their specialisation and type of school. These consist of the following eight areas:
- The organisation of education and its conditions, foundations of democracy
- Curriculum theory and didactics
- Theory of science, research methods and statistics
- Development and learning
- Special needs education
- Social relations, conflict management and leadership
- Assessment and grading
- Evaluation and development work (SOU 2008:109, p. 27)

The Inquiry conceives the above mentioned skills and knowledge as the core of educational science worth one year of full-time studies.

Level III comprises knowledge and skills specific to teachers in a certain age category or type of school. The Inquiry stresses the importance of "*good knowledge of the subject they teach*" and of the didactical perspective with regard to different subjects and student groups – "*subject didactics*".[27]

---

[27] The Inquiry HUT07 proposes a teacher education programme with a common core of educational science ("Utbildningsvetenskap") and a number of specialisations. Two new professional degrees, for primary school teachers and secondary school teachers, are proposed to replace the present single degree.

Quality of adult educators and the art of measuring something that is beautiful

Any systematic educational activity in which the State is involved includes elements of governance and control (Lindensjö & Lundgren (2005).

The control can be implemented either through rules or by targets. Governance by rules was replaced in the 1990s with overall objectives. As a result, the direct control of public business became indirect. The governance nowadays consists of monitoring and controlling target fulfillment through evaluation procedures and quality reports from all levels in educational institutions.

The responsibility to develop quality controlling instruments has to be placed at an operational level. Monitoring and evaluation processes in the hands of the operatives can serve as a tool for quality improvement, provided that they have sufficient knowledge of the complexity of learning processes and the possibility to reflect on *"how, for what purpose and for whom evaluations are made"*. The quality of educational environments should be a collective process in which the educators were directly involved and did participate on equal terms.

It is a process of participation, communication and reflection on the business and its development. Although it is difficult to define quality and perhaps even more difficult to measure, it does not discourage conscious work to make things better. Performance criteria and benchmarks may have their importance, but what ultimately seems to promote the quality of an educational activity is the ability of the organisation to create conditions for the participants' collective search for it. Operational self-governance and self-regulation means great opportunities for quality work. Staff, leadership and participants can develop their own methods of quality development and assurance that are better adapted and integrated in their pedagogical context.

Work with quality development occurs everywhere in human enterprises and no one seriously questions the importance of such work. Thus, the biggest problem has been the definition of quality in service-producing sectors in general and in public education in particular. The reason is that the "product" of such activities is people's subjective experiences of satisfaction with their educational needs. But let us examine what quality stands for and what possible meanings it might include.

Quality is usually defined as the opposite of *quantity* referring to the "nature" of something. Quality of an educational activity is something good - but what is that "good". Quality may be perceived to stand for either a way we approach a given task, the inherent value of the task or/ and an activity designed to do a task better. Awareness and knowledge of what quality is in an activity become extremely important today. But if we do not know what quality is, it is tricky to work to improve it.

Quality as a concept is at the heart of the discussion and its meaning depends on the context in which it appears. The word quality was rare in education policy texts before the 1990s, a period associated with a socio-ideological climate in which the liberal market thinking was totally hegemonic in every public sphere. New Public Management is the generic name for the new market economy inspired paradigm. (Karlsson Vestman & Andersson 2007; Nytell 2006; Strannegård 2007)

From the early 1990s quality became the signal word. Expressions such as quality control, quality assurance, quality development and quality assessment marked a paradigmatic shift in public discourse concerning the efficient production of goods and services. In particular, the inception of the concept of quality in education indicates the point of departure for a "new regime" of central management and control of publicly funded activities.

Nevertheless, quality is difficult to measure because it lacks visible references. This should not prevent us from trying to find ways to measure it. A definition to consider is e.g. the following:

> *We define quality as a measurable characteristic of producing services which makes it possible to rank producers according to how well they can meet the officially agreed norms.*[28]

However, a *bildning* ("bildung") process includes qualitative aspects that are elusive in distinct scales. Usually they remain unexplored, and thus invisible. The core of this problem can be illustrated by the following reflection from Antoine de Saint-Exupéry's *The Little Prince*:

---

28 Quoted by Susanne Weinberg (1995). "Kvalitetsmätningar – Ett verktyg eller ett otyg?". In: *På jakt efter sanningen. Om kvalitetsmätning och utvärdering.* Lärarförbundet, s. 18.

If I have told you these details about the asteroid, and made a note of its number for you, it is on account of the grown-ups and their ways. When you tell them that you have made a new friend, they never ask you any questions about essential matters. They never say to you, *"What does his voice sound like? What games does he love best? Does he collect butterflies?"* Instead, they demand: *"How old is he? How many brothers has he? How much does he weigh? How much money does his father make?"* Only from these figures do they think they have learned anything about him. If you were to say to the grown-ups: *"I saw a beautiful house made of rosy brick, with geraniums in the windows and doves on the roof,"* they would not be able to get any idea of that house at all. You would have to say to them: *"I saw a house that cost $20,000."* Then they would exclaim: *"Oh, what a pretty house that is!"*

(...)

They are like that. One must not hold it against them. Children should always show great forbearance toward grown-up people."[29]

Adult educators' competences and their quality: Research in progress

Current concepts as lifelong learning, professionalization, qualification, validation, quality assurance, competencies etc., used in various policy documents, seem to interrelate in a specific way. They constitute a prevailing discourse - an articulated set of certain beliefs of the role of education in the making of the virtuous citizen. The policy documents are interconnected to each other like links in a chain. It is important to identify the voices heard in the discourse and reveal the assumptions and power claims (agenda) behind the authoritative as well as normative utterances addressing the public and telling what is good for everyone.

Everything one does has the ultimate goal of what is good, or happiness. Bildning/Bildung has its objectives regardless of where it proceeds. These objectives can be either the ultimate aim of our actions or be embedded in actions. The latter constitutes durable processes that the con-

---

[29] Antoine de Saint-Exupéry: *The Little Prince* (http://www.odaha.com/littleprince.php?f=English)

cept adult learning is designed to capture and describe. Adult learning activities are undertaken not primarily, at least not directly, towards measured learning outcomes (knowledge as a product) which normally is the destination of the productive skills. Adult education's self-conception is that of dealing with knowledge and learning as an active process not decided (fixed) in advance. Identification, though, of learning actions that lead to the realization of the aims of a given education programme requires a determination of the aims in question. It also requires a determination of the qualifications and skills – competencies – educators need in order to help participants realize their educational needs.

What kind of competences adult educators need to develop is dependent on how clearly defined the concept of competence is and what the aims of different adult education activities are. What should the notion "adult educator", as indicating a broad range of individuals with the common characterization "one who helps adults learn", include of essential knowledge, abilities (competences, skills), attitudes and qualifications?

It is not so easy to talk about the adult educator as something fixed and ready or a product from a specific training programme delimited in time and space. It would be more appropriate to talk about the adult educator as a *species under development.*

The adult educator is a species in the making. It would make more sense to approach the nature of the adult educator's competence profile by inventing (constructing) developmental models of the same character as when trying to make sense of the development of human beings. A good start is to begin to identify adult educators' skills as manifested in the adult education field's various contexts, such as the EU-funded project Q2Teach are doing. Bringing together the results of the participating EU countries' Delphi-surveys will hopefully broaden our understanding of what adult educators know or should know, to facilitate adult learners' learning of good quality.

Undoubtedly, it takes time to become an adult educator in the sense that it takes time to develop the kind of potential ethics, in the Aristotelian sense, consisting of intellectual and moral abilities - *virtues*[30] – which

---

30 The virtue of something, according to Aristotle (*Nicomachean Ethics,* Book VI), is its proper excellence. It is a habitual way of acting, not an emotion or a capacity,

puts a man/a woman in position to recognize in others or help others to realize their capacities, needs and life dreams.

References

Andersson, E. (2001). *Cirkelledarskapet. En intervju- och enkätstudie med cirkelledare.* [Study Circle Leadership. An interview and questionnaire study with study circle leaders]. Stockholm: Folkbildningsrådet

Andersson, E. (2006). "Studiecirkeln – en idé om ett kollektivt självbildningsarbete". [The study circle - the idea of a collective self-education activity]. In: Borgström, Lena & Gougoulakis, Petros (eds.). *Vuxenantologin - En grundbok om vuxnas lärande.* Stockholm: Atlas Akademi, pp. 121-152

Andersson, P. (2006). Vuxenpedagogisk forskning i Sverige [Adult Education Research in Sweden]. In: Borgström, Lena & Gougoulakis, Petros (eds.). *Vuxenantologin - En grundbok om vuxnas lärande.* Stockholm: Atlas Akademi, pp. 73-118

Antoine de Saint-Exupéry: *The Little Prince* (http://www.odaha.com/littleprince.php?f=English)

Aristoteles (2004). Den nikomachiska etiken. [*Nicomachean Ethics*]. Göteborg: Daidalos

Borgström, L., Gougoulakis, P., Höghielm, R. (1998). *Lärande i studiecirkel. En studie av en pedagogisk miljö.* [Learning in study circle. A study of an educational milieu]. Lärarhögskolan i Stockholm

Bron-Wojciechowska, A. (1996) *Hur vuxna lär – pedagogiska perspektiv.* [How adults learn – pedagogical perspektctives]. In: Aribsson, G. & Kilbom, Å. (eds.). *Arbete efter 45. Historiska, psykologiska och fysiologiska perspektiv på äldre i arbetslivet.* [Work after 45. Historical, psykological and physiological perspectives on elderly people in working life]. Stockholm: Arbetslivsinstitutet.

Carlgren, I., Handal, G. & Sveinung, V., Eds. (1994). *Teachers' minds and ac-

---

in combination with an excellent rational thinking (idea). Aristotle's Virtues consist of moral virtues (about character) and intellectual virtues (about thinking). The intellectual virtues, identified by Aristotle, are perceived as different ways the soul takes to arriving at truth. They are grouped in:

a. **Theoretical virtues** (***Nous***: intuitive understanding, ***Episteme***: scientific knowledge, ***Sophia***: philosophical wisdom)
b. **Productive virtues** (***Techne***: skills)
c. **Practical virtues** (***Phronesis***: practical wisdom, sensibility, prudence)

tions: research on teachers' thinking and practice. London: The Falmer Press
Commission of the European Communities (2000). *A Memorandum on Lifelong Learning.* (http://www.bologna-berlin2003.de/pdf/MemorandumEng.pdf)
Commission of the European Communities (2005). *Proposal for a Recommendation of the European Parliament and of the Council on key competences for lifelong learning.* Brussels, 2005/0221(COD), COM(2005)548 (http://ec.europa.eu/education/policies/2010/doc/keyrec_en.pdf). [Accessed 19 April 2009]
Cross, J. (2007). *Informal Learning: Rediscovering the Natural Pathways That Inspire Innovation and Performance.* San Francisco: John Wiley & Sons, Inc.
Deer Richardson, L. & Wolfe, M. (eds.) (2001). *Principles and Practice of Informal Education: Learning Through Life.* New York: Routledge Falmer.
Docherry, P. (1996). *Läroriket – vägar och vägval i en lärande organisation* [The empire of learning – roads and crossroads within a learning organisation]. Solna: Arbetslivsinstitutet
Ekholm, M. (2007). Lärare, professionalitet och yrkeskvalitet [Teachers, professionalism and professional quality]. In: *Lärarprofessionalism – om professionella lärare.* Lärarförbundet, p. 6-19
Ellström P.-E. (1996) "Rutin och reflektion" [Routine and reflection]. In: *Livslångt lärande,* Ellström P.-E., Gustavsson, B., Larsson, S. (eds.). Studentlitteratur. Lund, pp. 142-179
Ellström, P.-E. (1992), *Kompetens, utbildning och lärande i arbetslivet. Problem, begrepp och teoretiska perspektiv.* [Skills, training and learning in the workplace. Problems, conceptual and theoretical perspectives]. Stockholm: Publica
Englund, T. (2007). Professionella lärare? [Professional teachers?] In: *Lärarprofessionalism – om professionella lärare.* Lärarförbundet, p. 78-99
European Communities (2008). *The European Qualifications Framework for Lifelong Learning (EQF).* Luxembourg: Office for Official Publications of the European Communities Available at: http://ec.europa.eu/dgs/education_culture/publ/pdf/eqf/broch_en.pdf [Accessed 19 April 2009]
Folkesson, L. (2005). Yrkesutbildning - och sedan? [Vocational education - and then?] In: Claes-Göran Wenestam & Birgit Lendahls Rosendahl (red). *Lärande i vuxenlivet.* Lund: Studentlitteratur, p. 67-98
Fullan, M. & Hargreaves, A. (1992). *Teacher development and educational change.* London: The Falmer Press
German Institute for Adult Education (2009). *Qualified to Teach - QF2TEACH.* Lifelong Learning Programme LEONARDO DA VINCI. Submission number: 504172-LLP-1-2009-1 CZ-GRUNDTVIG-GMP Available at: http://

ec.europa.eu/dgc/eduction_and_culture [Accessed 19 April 2009]
Goodson, Ivor F. (2005). Vad är professionell kunskap? - Förändrade värderingar av lärares yrkesroll [Professional Knowledge, Professional Lives. Studies in Education and Change.] Lund: Studentlitteratur.
Gougoulakis, P. (2006) *Bildning och lärande – om folkbildningens pedagogik.* [Bildning and learning – on the pedagogy of Popular Adult Education]. Stockholm: ABF
Gougoulakis, P., Bogataj, N. (2007). "Study Circles in Sweden and Slovenia – Learning for Civic Participation". In: Frane Adam (ed.), *Social Capital and Governance, Old and New Members of the EU in Comparison*, s. 203-236, Berlin: Lit Verlag
Gougoulakis, Petros (2001). *Studiecirkeln: Livslångt lärande ... på svenska! En icke-formell mötesplats för samtal och bildning för alla.* [The Study Circle: Lifelong learning ... in Swedish! A non-formal meeting place for discussion and learning for all]. HLS Förlag (PhD thesis)
Henschke, John A. (1998). " Modeling the Preparation of Adult Educators". In: *Spring, Volume 9, The Training of Adult Educators, Number 3, pp. 11-13.*
Hoskins, B. & Fredriksson, U. (2008). *Learning to Learn: What is it and can it be measured?* European Commission, Joint Research Centre, Institute for the Protection and Security of the Citizen, Centre for Research on Lifelong Learning (CRELL). ISBN: 978-92-79-09491-0
HSV (Högskoleverket) 2005:17 R. *Evaluation of the new teacher-training programmes at higher education institutions.* [National Agency for Higher Education]
Karlsson Vestman, O. & Andersson, Inger M. (2007). *Pedagogisk utvärdering som styrning – En historia från präster till PISA.* [Pedagogical Evaluation as governing - A story from the priests to PISA]. Myndigheten för skolutveckling, Forskning i fokus, nr 35;
Kelchtermans, G. (1993). Teachers and their Career Story. A Biographical Perspective on Professional Development. I: Christopher Day, James Calderhead & Pam Denicolo (eds.). *Research on teacher thinking understanding professional development.* London: The Falmer Press
Knowles, M.S. (1990). *The adult learner: A neglected species* (Revised Edition. Houston: Gulf Publishing Company
Kugel, P. (1993). How professors develop as teachers. In: *Studies in Higher Education,* 18, 3, pp. 315-328.
Larsson, S. (2006). *Didaktik för vuxna – tankelinjer i internationell litteratur.* [Didactics for adults - lines of thinking in international literature] Vetenskapsrådets rapportserie (12:2006)

Liedman, S.-E. (2008). *Nycklar till ett framgångsrikt liv? – Om EU:s nyckelkompetenser.* [Keys for a successful life? – About the EU's key competences]. Skolverket

Lindensjö, Bo & Lundgren, Ulf P. (2005). *Utbildningsreformer och politisk styrning.* HLS förlag.

Linstone, Harold A. & Turoff, M., eds. (2002). The *Delphi Method. Techniques and Applications.* Available in digital version: http://www.is.njit.edu/pubs/delphibook/ [Accessed 19 April 2009]

Lpf 94. *Curriculum for the non-compulsory school system.* Available at: http://www.skolverket.se/publikationer?id=1072 [Accessed 19 April 2009]

Nuissl, E. & Lattke, S., eds. (2008). *Qualifying adult learning professionals in Europe.* Bielefeld: W. Bertelsmann Verlag GmbH & Co

Nytell, H. (2006): *Från kvalitetsidé till kvalitetsregim: Om statlig styrning av skolan.* [From a quality idea to a quality regime. On state governing of the school]. Uppsala Universitet: Humanistisk-samhällsvetenskapliga vetenskapsområdet.

OECD (2005). *The Definition and Selection of Competencies (DeSeCo). Executive Summary.* Available at: http://www.oecd.org/dataoecd/47/61/35070367.pdf [Accessed 19 April 2009]

OECD *Definition and Selection of Key Competencies* (DeSeCo) *: Executive Summary.* Availbale at: http://www.oecd.org/dataoecd/47/61/35070367.pdf [Accessed 19 April 2009]

Proctor, R.W. and Dutta, A. (1995). *Skill Acquisition and Human Performance,* London: Sage.

Regeringens proposition 1997/98:115. *Folkbildning* [Government Bill]

Regeringens proposition 1999/2000:135. *En förnyad lärarutbildning.* [A renewed teacher education]. Utbildningsdepartementet.

Regeringens proposition 2005/06:192 *Lära, växa, förändra.* [Learn, grow, change]. Regeringens folkbildningsproposition.

Rychen, D.S. & Tiana, A. (2004), *Developing Key Competencies in Education: Some Lessons from International and National Experience,* Geneva: UNESCO-IBE, Studies in Comparative Education.

Schön, D. (1983). *The Reflective Practioner: How Professionals Think in Action.* Basic Books, New York

SOU 1996:159. *Folkbildningen - en utvärdering.* [Adult education – an evaluation].Slutbetänkande av utredningen för statlig utvärdering av folkbildningen. Stockholm: Fritzes.

SOU 2000:28. *Kunskapsbygget 2000 - det livslånga lärandet.* [Knowledge Construction 2000 - lifelong learning]. Utbildningsdepartementet: Kunskapslyftskommittén

SOU 2004:30. *Folkbildning i brytningstid.* [Popular education in transition]. Slutbetänkande av Utredningen för statens utvärdering av folkbildningen (SUFO 2). Utbildningsdepartementet

SOU 2008:109. *En hållbar lärarutbildning* [Sustainable teacher education]. Betänkande av Utredningen om en ny lärarutbildning (HUT07)

Strannegård, L., red., (2007). *Den omätbara kvaliteten.* [The immeasurable quality]. Norstedts Akademiska Förlag.

Tiana, A. (2004) *Developing key competencies in education systems: some lessons from international studies and national experiences.* In Rychen, D.S. & Tiana, A. (Eds.) *Developing key competencies in education: some lessons form international and national experiences.* Geneva: UNESCO / International Bureau of Education.

Weinberg, S. (1995). "Kvalitetsmätningar – Ett verktyg eller ett otyg?". [Quality Measurement - A tool or a nuisance?]. In: *På jakt efter sanningen. Om kvalitetsmätning och utvärdering.* Lärarförbundet.

Winterton, J., Delamare-Le Deist, F. & Stringfellow, E. (2005). *Typology of knowledge, skills and competences: clarification of the concept and prototype.* Research report elaborated on behalf of Cedefop/Thessaloniki - Final draft. (CEDEFOP Project No RP/B/BS/Credit Transfer/005/04)

Zhou Nan-Zhao: *Four 'Pillars of Learning' for the Reorientation and Reorganization of Curriculum: Reflections and Discussions.* Available at: http://www.ibe.unesco.org/fileadmin/user_upload/COPs/Pages_documents/Competencies/Further_Reading/PillarsLearningZhou.pdf [Accessed 19 April 2009]

The framing of collaboration and its impact on creativity and innovative skills

Birthe Lund and Annie Aarup Jensen

Introduction

The European Parliament and the EU Education, Youth and Culture Council have proclaimed the year 2009 to be the European Year of Creativity and Innovation, in order to raise public awareness of the significance of creativity and innovation in today's knowledge society. This poses a challenge to all educational systems, including Higher Education.

Conceptualising how it is possible to develop *new* knowledge - knowledge building and knowledge transmission - is an essential element of all learning theories. Knowledge may be understood as a property or *capacity of an individual mind* or examined as a *process of participation in various cultural practices*. The first understanding of knowledge creation as a capacity of the individual mind tends to focus on cognition and processes of knowledge creation. The second understanding of knowledge building examines learning as a process of participation in various cultural practices and in shared learning activities such as project work. Here, cognition and knowledge is viewed as distributed across both the individual and the environment, and learning is regarded as *situated* in relations. Consequently, learning becomes a matter of participation in practice and actions.

We assume that the understanding of how we learn is closely related to the understanding of the pedagogical processes regarding the development of creativity. If we regard learning as a matter of participation it becomes relevant to focus on stimulating and motivating participation within an educational setting in order to create new knowledge and innovation through group work.

We are theoretically inspired by J. Bruner (1996), who emphasises the importance of interaction, learning culture and self-development, and sees learning as both an individual and a collective process that is situated in a specific culture. In this respect transmission of knowledge is a social phenomenon. Learning is regarded as an active process in which the students construct their knowledge, and we assume that the quality of the knowledge construction process is dependent on how the processes are framed, structured and designed. Since the educational system at all levels expects that innovation can be taught, it is relevant to explore if there are any pedagogical strategies that may stimulate creativity and innovation in groups at university level. While there has been much research on individual creativity and organisational innovation, little research has examined the combination of creativity, innovation and teamwork from a learning perspective.

Innovation is closely related to idea development, and therefore it is relevant to study *how creative ideas occur* within a group and explore pedagogical practices which may support creativity and thereby develop innovative competences.

We will examine the development of creativity and innovative competence within a frame of collaboration in relation to problem-solving and problem-finding. This is relevant since it is assumed that project-organised, problem-based learning may lead to creative students. At Aalborg University students are organised in project groups during most of their education, one semester at a time. This pedagogical organisation is – in its self-perception - characterised by active learner participation in collaborative problem-finding and problem-solving. The students are encouraged to regard the knowledge of fellow students as a resource and they are expected to define their own study task through group negotiations.

It is our hypothesis that this collaboration process may need "scaffolding" to support the development of innovative skills. The predominant pedagogical concept for improvement of innovative competence in Denmark is called KUBUS (Herlau & Tetzschner, 2006). Through the application of a set of tools, KUBUS aims at enhancing responsibility for own learning and the development of self-directed groups. KUBUS is a method and a language which makes management and decision processes visible. It is a method which may improve the students' skills in teambuilding, democratic decision-making processes, and entrepreneurship (Lund, 2007). In this chapter we will discuss how the KUBUS-concept may function as a scaffolding device in problem-oriented learning, since it has proven to be a big challenge for our students to manage the dynamic processes of collaboration and problem-formulation.

Problem-formulation in problem-oriented project work

Aalborg University was founded in 1974 and it is based on the pedagogical philosophy of problem-oriented learning, characterised by:

1. *Problem orientation*, which means that the point of departure is the subject-related knowledge, methods and theories relevant to the specific problem. Interdisciplinarity becomes a leading principle.
2. *Participant direction*, which means that both the definition of the problem and the choice of work methods must lie with the students as this is the only way to create the possibilities for accommodative learning processes necessary to develop creativity and flexibility. Furthermore, the problem in question has to be, and be experienced as, relevant for the individual student in order to ensure the appropriate learning process. As a consequence of this the principle of participation in decision making becomes important.
3. *The principle of exemplarity*, which means that working with important and representative aspects exemplify the area of the discipline in question.
4. *Group work*.
5. *The communicative didactics*, with primary focus on the forms of work and cooperation and the considerations regarding the choice of content. (Illeris, 1974)

As early as 1974 when the Danish educational researcher Knud Illeris (Illeris, 1974) formulated the principles of problem-oriented project work within the framework of experiential learning, he was aware of the creative / innovative qualifications which might be the outcome of problem-oriented learning. Referring to Piaget's cognitive theory of learning Illeris understands accommodative learning processes as the prerequisite for creativity.

Ideally, problem-oriented project work implies selection of subject or problem, formulation of problem, production (of project report), and product evaluation.

In problem-oriented learning the ability to formulate and answer the "good question" is essential. It is an important (but arduous) task to find a problem which is really regarded as relevant by all participants. Illeris emphasises that the time spent on discussion and negotiation is valuable as it contributes to the accommodative learning which is of decisive importance to the quality of both process and product. The process is supported by a supervisor who is an expert within the domain, but the organisation of the process is up to the students. It is our experience that a growing number of students end up working alone; this might be related to the fact that they find group work too time-consuming and inefficient.

The idea for the problem ideally arises based on problems and issues experienced by the students, but it may also stem from subjects presented as part of the study program courses. The idea or problem in question will be made concrete and defined through the group's dialogue and discussion.

In the instructional model outlined by Illeris the criteria for the good problem are primarily that the *problem is perceived to be essential and relevant to both the individual participant and all the participants*, i.e. common to all group members. In formulating the problem the students negotiate and independent opinion formation among the students may arise. Illeris stresses that it is important that the students cultivate a critical perspective in order to avoid mere reproduction of existing knowledge; instead they become open to the possibility of change. The students must be able to reflect on and critically consider the consequences of any proposed changes or interventions[31]. From their first semester through to their graduation the students are encouraged and expected to create new knowledge.

Figure 1 illustrates the phases of the project work, the interplay between the processes, and the input and support for the process, i.e., the scaffolding of the process.

---

31 K. Illeris was inspired by e.g. critical theory (The Frankfurt School).

Figure 1

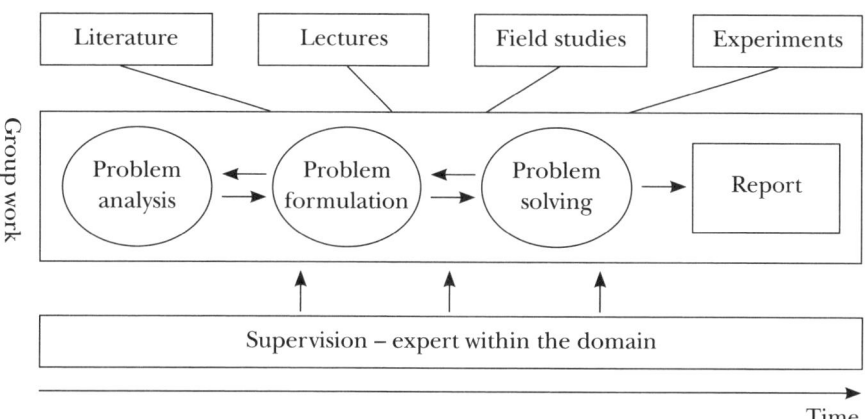

The time spent on discussion is assumed to contribute to the accommodative learning and lead to creative students, but we claim that such a development is closely related to how the students actually participate and collaborate and how the group process is supported.

The creative process and problem-finding

The term *"creativity"* is typically used to refer to the act of producing new ideas, approaches or actions, while *"innovation"* is the process of both generating and applying such creative ideas in some specific context. Since it is difficult to examine phenomena like creativity and innovation in relation to group work and collaboration from a pedagogical perspective, without discussing what is meant by creativity, we will briefly examine the concept of "creativity" and discuss how it may be related to creation as a social process.

Research that understands creativity as a personal attribution has identified key elements that characterise the creative person and operate with personality. It reflects certain personality or style factors – such as an *open mind, tolerance to ambiguity*, as well as some cognitive functions such as *ideational fluency and thinking flexibility* (e.g. Csikszentmihalyi, 1997). Along with identifying cognitive characteristics, Almeida et al. (2008) present some topics in order to reach a better definition of creativity as a *cognitive* characteristic:

1. it is more associated with divergent than convergent thinking and production
2. it is more an individual attribute than a universal or normative construct
3. it is more related to insight and novelty than to learning and routine behaviour
4. it may be characterized by problem-finding rather than problem-solving
5. it uses remote rather than spontaneous or frequent ideational association

These characteristics indicate that the authors regard creativity as closely related to divergent thinking, insight, novelty, problem-finding and ideational association. Such findings indicate that in order to develop creativity we must focus on development of *divergent thinking and problem-finding* which we see as closely related to experiential learning and a socio-cultural approach to creativity.

This socio-cultural approach to creativity indicates that creativity development requires understanding, not only of the individual inspiration and creativity, but also of social factors.

There exist at least two competitive theories about the creative process: *Idealist* theories which argue that once you have the "creative idea", the creative process is completed when the idea is fully formed in your head, and *action theories* which argue that *the execution of the creative work is essential* to the creative process. Action theorists deny that fully formed ideas emerge spontaneously from the subconscious mind of the creator. From this perspective, explanations of how and why insights suddenly occur are essential in creativity research and are related to creativity "myths".

Sawyer (2006) describes a 4-phased model including stages of creativity:

1. *Preparation*: The initial phase of preliminary work. Collecting data and information, searching for related ideas. An important part of the preparation involves becoming familiar with prior work and internalizing the symbols and conventions of the domain (in order to generate new contributions to creativity).
2. *Incubation*: The delay between preparation and the moment of insight. The prepared material is elaborated and organized internally.

The incubation stage is often below the surface of consciousness, and it is the stage that is the less understood in the creative process. During incubation mental elements combine, and insights occur when certain combinations emerge into consciousness. (Many creative people get their best insights during a period of idle time – gardening, or when working on other problems.)
3. *Insight*: It is the subjective experience of having an idea. In incubation, existing ideas are blended and combined to form complex mental structures; some of these mental structures surface into consciousness and are often referred to as "aha" moments. It is, with reference to Sawyer, unknown exactly how existing pieces of the domain mix together in the creator's mind.
4. *Verification*: Includes two sub-stages: evaluation and elaboration. After the insight emerges into consciousness, the creator has to evaluate the insight in order to determine the idea. The evaluation stage is fully conscious. After evaluation comes elaboration, conscious hard work, and in that phase the creator must use her/his immense domain of knowledge to convert the idea into a finished product/work. The creators usually experience a continued cycle of mini-insights and revision while elaborating on the insight.

Sawyer operates with neither curiosity nor questions as part of the preparation phase, nor does he discuss the motivation for joining a creative process. These processes are, however, regarded as the driving forces in project pedagogy.

Critics of this stage model claim that it is a little too linear – the creative process is more cyclical, since insights often generate even more questions than answers. A good question can be very valuable for further research and in science it often leads to reformulation of difficult problems. Along with this, Rothenberg (cited in Sawyer, 2006) argued that creation is not found in a single moment of insight, it is part of a long series of circumstances, often interrupted, reconstructed and repeated. Rothenberg points out that the temporal distinction between inspiration and elaboration in the creative process is incorrect, since the phases or functions alternate from start to finish (Sawyer 2006: 71). Especially the moment of insight is discussed, and Sawyer also claims that insight is overrated. He states that the typical creator experience is based on many small mini-insights every day, and that such insights can be traced back to the material on which the creators were consciously working. Creative activities require problem-solving and decision-making throughout the process, and each one of these decision points involves a small amount of creative inspiration.

Today many psychologists compare the stages of creativity to the stages of problem-solving and problem-finding. Though problem-solving and problem-finding is related, the big difference is that in problem-finding the problem is not known in advance but emerges from the process of the work itself through "small amounts of inspiration". From this theoretical perspective, problem-oriented group work, in which students take an active part in problem-finding, may generate creativity since the students are involved in all phases of the creative stages. Consequently, this means that special attention should be paid to how problem-finding and problem-solving are defined and supported pedagogically.

Recent research in the effects of conflict and dissent on creativity in groups (Troyer and Youngreen, 2009) shows that the form of feedback to group members' contributions, ideas etc. will have an impact on the creative performance of the group as a whole. It is the general impression that group-work is experienced as difficult, also because of the potential for conflicts inherent in this form of work. However, research has demonstrated that conflict in group work is crucial for the avoidance of 'group-thinking', which means that for fear of negative consequences, loss of status within the groups, etc., the individual group member refrains from voicing doubts or criticism regarding the group's work and decisions. Research has shown that negative evaluations from fellow group members are more likely to occur when ideas are presented than when facts are presented. In the extreme such a desire for group consensus may result in poor quality of the group product and dissent may therefore be a very valuable aspect in group work when it comes to quality enhancement. This constitutes a pedagogical challenge in relation to collaborative learning in particular and project-organised studies in general. Group climate and openness in relation to generation of ideas are issues of particular importance regarding the development of innovative abilities, and we therefore examined if there are other pedagogical techniques or tools which might minimize group-thinking and thus create more creative and innovative students.

KUBUS – supporting problem-finding?

We introduced the KUBUS concept (Herlau & Tetzschner, 2006) in order to examine whether such structures for the management of the group process would minimize the rate of conflicts related to group work and thereby increase the creativity level and innovation ability. KUBUS aims at supporting the creation of self-directed groups. It is expected that the group is self-managed, and KUBUS offers a number of different tools for group management. A KUBUS group communicate both internally and by external interactions. They have certain knowledge as well as uncertain knowledge and ignorance to deal with. A major challenge for the group is dealing with and sharing the uncertainty in a constructive way, regarding ignorance as a potential basis for knowledge building when it comes to developing innovation skills. By confronting this ignorance the group is challenged to reflect on what the group thinks it knows. To handle this KUBUS supports the creating of a group climate which allows for open questions and builds ways to communicate *knowledge potentials* based on ignorance. Over time ignorance will be reduced, or it is replaced with shared certainty related to documented knowledge.

The KUBUS model has been applied and tested in various settings as a didactic method for training entrepreneurship, and we wanted to test if this model could scaffold the problem-formulation phase and thereby support the students' collaborative and innovative skills which are important in project-work. The KUBUS concept has, in different versions, been introduced at colleges of education and at the upper secondary education level in previous years. The KUBUS model was developed by Henrik Herlau and is based on empirical case studies of how interdisciplinary groups (primarily student groups) worked in projects.

What is particularly interesting in this case is that KUBUS has special concerns for what in creativity terms would be described as a problem-finding phase. Herlau refers to this problem-finding phase as a *pre-ject phase*. While finding a problem a group often has to deal with considerable uncertainty related to "non-knowledge". KUBUS claims that this phase needs special management. It is characterised by being non-linear, divergent and process driven. It is a big challenge to collaborate without having a defined problem to solve, so students tend to avoid this situation by rushing into the problem-solving phase too early and they often define the problem without being fully aware of "the missing knowledge". KUBUS is developed to deal with problems – also problems not yet regarded as problems. *Problem-finding* in complex situations is dependent on both knowledge and *problem-framing*. In self-directed group work students have to negotiate, discuss and challenge the other group members' framing of the problems. The lack of a goal concerns a dynamic phase of problem identification; problem framing and re-framing (Herlau & Tetzschner, 2006). That is why problem-finding and problem-definition is also a question of "ownership" to the project. Those who define the problem own the project in problem-oriented project-work.

The general idea of the 'pre-ject' phase is to gather as much information and gain as much knowledge as possible before deciding on the action to take, whether it should be to discard that line of work or whether to pursue it further. In this way the KUBUS concept draws attention to the dynamic and reiterative process of generating ideas as a part of problem-finding.

It is important to train the participants' awareness of the pre-ject phase focus on uncertainty management, and KUBUS therefore operates with two leadership functions which all members of the group occupy by turns. One leader-role is task-oriented and focuses on outcome and responsibility for decision-making, and the other leader-role is relation-oriented and responsible for process, group climate, creativity and social interaction. The group draws up a social codex on the norms of behaviour, stating their mutual expectations regarding contribution, group participation, behaviour etc. This codex made in group consensus combined with the clear distribution of leadership roles means that there is a basis for performing transparent leadership. In this way group-members get to understand the role of the decision maker as well as the role of the person in charge of the group climate, and they ideally understand the necessity of being or becoming 'leadable', i.e. accepting the decisions of the group and of the leader and contributing to the group's work.

The group's work is highly documented through the use of a database (the 'Template') giving the group a general overview of the task and its progression, and providing an important transparency for the group members regarding the distribution of assignments and their completion. The continuous documentation, coupled with the fact that all ideas are preserved, makes it possible to return to a previous stage in the process and reconsider the options. Through the Template the supervisor is able to follow the process.

THE FRAMING OF COLLABORATION 155

Figure 2 illustrates the phases of the process and the scaffolding elements of the KUBUS concept.

Figure 2

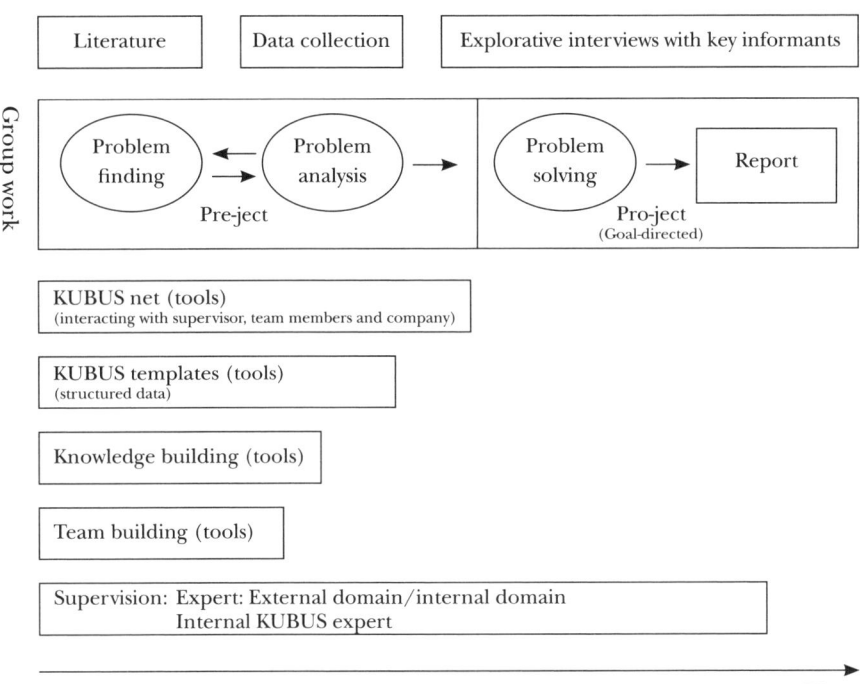

In this concept the supervisor has a more unobtrusive role in the process and she is not necessarily an expert within a knowledge domain. The focus is on developing the students' capacity to collaborate and manage the knowledge building process.

Students at the master program in Learning and Innovative Change at Aalborg University participated in an experiment using KUBUS and were afterwards interviewed. A KUBUS course usually runs for a year; our experiment, however, was a 'light' version of the concept, running for 4 weeks and focusing on the pre-ject phase (problem-finding). In this phase the students did not have other assignments. They were connected to either a company or a school and they examined these institutions in order to explore new possibilities for development and new markets.

The results of our interviews with the students emphasise how KUBUS influenced the students' interaction and created a new learning culture which gave room for new self-development. KUBUS stimulated an active learning process in which the students constructed their knowledge in interaction with 'the real world' by working with problems related to existing companies and institutions. They would create new ideas or find new ways of conceptualising problems and thus create new challenges for the involved stakeholders by defining their problems from unexpected and untraditional angles. In this way their innovative capabilities were trained.

The informants stated that the work undertaken within these formal structures proved productive, with the added benefit that all the work processes became very transparent for the participants. In the Template it was easy to see who was responsible for what, and the structures supported the knowledge sharing and knowledge building processes. In this way they could be explicit about their work process through their use of the Template and they were provided with a vocabulary for addressing the individual elements of the process (roles, phases, tasks, fields of research, etc.). The system indicated how much time was spent on each task, which in itself was time-reducing and left more time for idea-generating processes. The effectiveness of the meetings left more space for the individual's data collection, studies and research.

We observed that it was a challenge for the students to stay in the zone of uncertainty and ignorance and construct possible questions that further exposed their lack of knowledge to each other instead of formulating questions within a knowledge domain they knew about. In this way the KUBUS tools helped the students remain in the problem-*finding* phase. At the same time they experienced that lack of knowledge could be regarded as a resource and that it left room for playing with ideas.

The good problem-formulation in problem-oriented project work is characterised by being related to a specific knowledge domain and to the fact that it is answerable. Therefore, it was a challenge to the students to formulate questions which were not founded in specific knowledge domains they already knew, as intended in the pre-ject phase of the KUBUS concept.

The students emphasise that KUBUS affects the group climate in a positive way, making people less afraid of saying something, and it releases energy, creating the possibility for a more *playful* atmosphere within the group allowing 'small amounts of inspiration' to take place.

Research has demonstrated (Troyer and Youngreen, 2009) that creativity is higher in circumstances where negative evaluations are de-personalised, i.e. expressed as an evaluation of the idea rather than an evaluation of the person putting the idea forward, and participants report that working in an environment where evaluations take that form is more satisfactory. These research findings are corroborated by the statements from the informants in our case study. De-personalisation of the feedback and the evaluation allows for the critical stance which is necessary in order to enhance quality in the professional work, and it circumvents the social considerations which might prevent the members from voicing objections. On the other hand it provides the space for idea generation as the fear of loss of face, loss of social status etc. within the group is reduced correspondingly.

The informants in our case report that they were surprised to discover the degree to which they felt the urge to close the problem-finding phase in order to go into the problem-solving phase. With reference to Kruglanski (1989), Chirumbolo et al. define the need for (non-specific) cognitive closure as a desire for a definite answer to a question, any firm answer, rather than uncertainty, confusion, or ambiguity. The need for closure may be increased in situations where information processing becomes unpleasant or difficult due to e.g. time pressure, noise or mental fatigue. However, other factors may relieve the need for closure, for instance when focus is put on either the costs of premature closure or the potential benefits of delaying closure (Chirumbolo et al.). Examples of the costs in relation to our case may be that the project-group is afraid of making the wrong decisions and thus risks basing their work on invalid premises. Examples of the benefits may be the promises of receiving favourable evaluations due to a very solid or innovative and well-thought-through project. When the need for closure manifests itself in a group, the result has been demonstrated to be that fewer hypotheses are generated and there will be a "tendency to seize and freeze on an early, plausible hypothesis" (Chirumbolo et al.: 62), and in this respect reduce creativity.

Scaffolding creativity development

Since we regard the relationship between problem-finding and problem-solving as essential in creativity development view we regard KUBUS as a didactical tool for scaffolding creativity development since it insists on the differentiation between the pre-ject and the project phase. In this way it pays special attention to problem-finding (without using this term). It combines the different interactions in a creative process which relates creativity to problem-finding and problem-solving instead of looking at creativity from an idealistic perspective which pays special attention to the illumination – 'the magic moment' – when the perfect idea suddenly pops up without anyone being aware of how it is settled in a social process of gathering knowledge and small loops of problem-solving.

Group climate and social relations are important for the quality of the later problem-solving process. In this respect KUBUS becomes relevant since it claims that innovation processes demand a special kind of management which is different from the management of goal-oriented projects by insisting on nursing the social climate of the group by splitting up group leadership into two functions and indicating the difference between process-oriented management and goal-oriented management. Here we see a parallel between the innovation strategy of the KUBUS concept and the idea generation of the problem-finding phase of the problem-oriented project work. There is a big difference between the ability to answer an already formulated question and the ability to find and define a relevant question. So, an important part of developing creativity is about making room and a group climate which supports self-defined tasks/assignments. Problem-oriented work supports knowledge development and learning through its insistence on problem-formulation as a common ground for collaboration. In order to avoid that this process develops into a battlefield there is a need for shared rules of collaboration and interaction. The process of defining the rules (codes of conduct) is scaffolded in KUBUS via the dual management system.

One didactic potential is that KUBUS visualises each group member's contribution and her involvement in group processes and tasks, and this transparency may expose a participant's lack of involvement in the process at an early stage. It reduces the possibility to be a 'sleeping partner' and offers a framework for addressing such sensitive issues without damaging the group climate. If the management elements of KUBUS are successfully integrated into the problem-oriented project work it might scaffold the process and contribute to each member's commitment and active participation in the entire learning process, from problem-finding to problem-formulation and problem-solving and in this way foster innovative skills.

References

Almeida, L. S., Prieto, L. P., Ferrando, M., Oliveira, E. and Ferrándiz, C. (2008) Torrance Test of Creative Thinking: The question of its construct validity. In: *Thinking Skills and Creativity* p. 1871-1871 vol:3 iss:1 p. 53

Amabile, Teresa M.; Barsade, Sigal G.; Mueller, Jennifer S.; Staw, Barry M., "Affect and creativity at work," *Administrative Science Quarterly*, 2005, vol. 50, p. 367–403.

Bruner, J. (1996) *The Culture of Education,* Harvard University Press.

Chirumbolo, Antonio; Mannetti, Lucia; Pierro, Antonio; Areni, Alessandra; Kruglanski, Arie W. (2005) Motivated Closed-Mindedness and Creativity in Small Groups. *Small Group Research.* Vol. 36 No. 1, February 2005 59-82, Sage Publications.

Csikszentmihalyi, M. (1997) *Creativity. Flow and the psychology of discovery and invention.* Harper Perennial.

Darsø, L. (2001) *Innovation in the Making.* Samfundslitteratur.

Herlau H., Tetzschner, H. (2006) *Kubuskonceptet – prejektledelse og innovation.* Forlaget Samfundslitteratur.

Illeris, K. (1974) *Problem orientation and participant direction. An introduction to alternative didactics.* København: Munksgaard.

Keller, R.T. (1988) Predictors of the performance of project groups in R & D organizations. *Academy of Management Journal. Vol. 29, No. 4,* 715-726.

Kjærsdam, F. and Enemark, S. (1994). *The Aalborg Experiment – project innovation in university education,* Aalborg: Aalborg University Press.

Kolmos, A., Fink, F.K., Krogh, L. (2004) *The Aalborg PBL model. Progress, Diversity and Challenges.* Aalborg: Aalborg University Press.

Lund, B. (2010) Innovation Strategies in School (pp. 39-52) in K. Skogan/J. Sjøvoll (eds.) Creativity and Innovation. Preconditions for entrepreneual Education, Tapir Academic Press, Tronheim.

Lund, B. (2008) Innovation og kreativitetsudvikling. *Kognition og pædagogik, nr. 69,* September 2008, *18. årgang.*

Lund, B. (2007) Jagten på den innovative didaktik. Downloaded: http://www.

abcinnovation.dk/uploads/Jagten%20p%E5%20den%20innovative%20 didaktik%20-%20Birthe%20Lund.pdf

Mansfield, R.S., Busse, T. V., Krepelka, E.J. (1978) Effectiveness of Creativity Training. *Review of Educational Research* vol. 48 no. 4 autumn pp. 517 – 536

Paulus, P.B. (2000) Groups, Teams, and Creativity: The Creative Potential of Idea-generating Groups. In *Applied Psychology: An International Review, 49 (2)*, 237-262.

Pirola-Merlo, A. and Mann, L. (2004) The relationship between individual creativity and team creativity: aggregating across people and time. In: *Journal of Organizational Behaviour. 25*, 235-257.

Savery, J.R. & Duffy, T.M. (2001) *Problem Based Learning: An instructional model and its constructivist framework.* CRLT Technical Report No. 16-01. Indiana University. June.

Sawyer, R.K. (2006) *Explaining Creativity – the Science of Human Innovation.* Oxford: Oxford University Press.

Stako, A.J. (2001) *Creativity in the Classroom.* Lawrence Erlbaum Associates Publishers, Mahwah New Jersey.

Troyer, L. and Youngreen, R. (2009) Conflict and Creativity in Groups. In: *Journal of Social Issues, Vol. 65, No. 2,* p. 409–427.

West, M.A. and Wallace, M. (1991) Innovation in Health care teams. *European Journal of Social Psychology. Vol. 21,* 303-315.

Teacher Teams as (De-)Professionalizing?
– Possible consequences of the 2005 Reform in the Danish Upper Secondary School

Thomas R. S. Albrechtsen & Dion Rüsselbæk Hansen

Introduction

The continual professional development of teachers is often seen as a positive and desirable goal.[32] Teachers are – like many other working adults today – described as "lifelong learners" who are more or less destined to develop new competencies and to keep up with new developments in a knowledge-based society. Today, lifelong learning is a "fate", not a choice. Teachers often engage in organized continual learning,[33] but how, what and why something must be learned varies and depends on the particular circumstances, dominant discourses and cultural contexts.

Inspired by this widely held ideal of lifelong learning a new reform for the upper secondary school was passed by the Danish parliament in 2003, and the implementation process began in August 2005. When we are referring to the Danish Upper Secondary Reform, we are using the term *Reform 2005*. Contrary to the Danish primary schools where the teachers have worked in teacher teams since the nineties, it has not been the case in the Danish upper secondary schools. Whereas, for instance, the Danish primary teachers generally are very familiar with pedagogical issues, the Danish upper secondary teachers have always been very attached to their teaching subjects. Pedagogical issues have never been dominant factors for the upper secondary teachers as they have for the Danish primary teachers.

---

32 European Commission 2004.
33 Day 1999, p. 1.

A typical Danish upper secondary teacher has a master's degree in one or two subjects. To be able to teach in a Danish upper secondary school a teacher must also complete a course in educational theory and practice, called "Pædagogikum", before or subsequent to their appointment at the school.[34] Often this course takes one year. Despite these qualifications, the Danish Upper Secondary teachers are often criticized for their lack of pedagogical understanding. Most teachers identify themselves with their university subject(s) and often work alone with their subjects and their classes.[35]

One of the intentions of Reform 2005 is to change this situation. The former Danish minister of education, Ulla Tørnæs,[36] argued that changes in the upper secondary schools are needed if the government's stated aims are to be reached by 2015. One of the government's aims is to include 95 percent of young people in the youth education system.

In Denmark the educational system consists of nine years of compulsory education. After finishing compulsory school, the students can continue their education choosing between different kinds of upper secondary schools. In this paper we are only referring to the part of the Danish Upper Secondary School that is called "The Gymnasium (stx)".[37]

To facilitate Reform 2005 upper secondary school teachers in The Gymnasium have to focus on developing several new competencies. For instance, teachers must work in *teacher teams* and be able to carry out complex pedagogical reflections. The team idea challenges the teacher's "freedom of method". It is seen as a way to facilitate teachers' desires to develop a stronger collective culture so they will be able to manage the increasing demands placed upon individual teachers[38].

Despite these great intentions, several questions emerge: What do the new demands mean? Do the teachers develop new professional competencies during their work in teams? What problems may have emerged through Reform 2005?

---

34 The Danish Ministry of Education 2009.
35 Damberg et al. 2006 and Lading 2006.
36 Tørnæs 2004.
37 See the Danish Ministry of Education 2009, *Upper Secondary Education. The Gymnasium (STX)*.
38 Beck & Hansen 2009.

Our aim in this paper is to discuss the following:

How may the implementation of teacher teams be said to be contributing to either professionalism or de-professionalism among Danish upper secondary teachers?

On the basis of the 2003 reform document and our theoretical engagement with *discourses on modernization, professionalism and the intensification of teacher's work, we are focusing on the possible consequences of the implementation of teacher teams* in the Danish upper secondary schools. First, we will discuss how modernization influences the field. Second, we will focus on how professionalism is understood among teacher teams. Third, we will focus on the possible consequences of the implementation of teacher teams.

Tendencies of modernization in the Danish Upper Secondary School

During the last decade the Danish Ministry of Education has written several reform documents related to Danish Upper Secondary Schools. Based on these ideas the Upper Secondary Reform was launched in 2005.[39] Today the teacher must be creative and perform interesting teaching with the goal of strengthening students' knowledge, proficiency and competencies. The goal is to develop creative, innovative and active students. Reform 2005 assumes that the development of the students' creative and innovative competencies prepares citizens for future challenges in knowledge-based society.

One year after the implementation of Reform 2005, the Danish Government launched an ambitious and pro-active strategy. In the report *Progress Innovation and Cohesion - Strategy for Denmark in the Global Economy* (2006) it is pointed out that everyone must participate in the renewal process if there is to be progress and cohesion. Again, as in the 2005 reform, it is stated that the teacher plays a key role in this process.[40] In fact, it is often claimed that the teachers' personal and creative qualities have a significant impact on students' achievements and educational

---

39 The Danish Ministry of Education. *The Upper Secondary School Reform 2003.*
40 The Danish Government 2006, see: *www.globalisering.dk/multimedia/Pixi_UK_web_endelig1.pdf.*

improvement.[41] If we follow Beck and Beck-Gernsheim's[42] reasoning this can partly be explained by the increased individualization and reflexivity in modern societies. Teachers, now more than ever, are expected to compete, perform, be creative and make individual as well as collective judgments and evaluations.[43] Today, it is not enough for teachers to give reasons for decisions and judgments based on some general rules, traditions, habits or routines. As Bauman puts it:

> "Postmodern humans are denied the luxury of assuming, with Shakespearean hero, that there is a method in this madness. If the habits acquired in the course of training prompt them to seek such cohesive and coherent structures and make their actions depend on finding them – they are in real trouble"[44]

In light of this, we argue that a new creative ethos emerges. Today, the ideal teacher is considered to be *creative*. We understand creativity as an ability to see things differently and consider new perspectives, ideas, and solutions that sometimes include creating new vocabularies. This tendency can also be read out of the Upper Secondary Reform document.[45] It means that the upper secondary teacher must strive to use a wide range of creative teaching strategies to develop their practice and be able to act wisely in the concrete context.

We use the term *wisely* to indicate, that we are not just speaking about skills and technique (technical know-how). Instead we are speaking about teachers' ethical actions (ethical know-how)[46] set alongside their understanding of student's needs and interests.[47] From this point of view it is the teacher's responsibility to devise how the students achieve the

---

41 Cochran-Smith 2004; Prosser & Trigwell 2001.
42 Beck and Beck-Gernsheim 2001.
43 There is an increased competition going on among the Danish upper secondary schools. Now, the schools have to compete to get students. To be able to attract students, it is required that the schools promote themselves. For instance, they can offer creative and special learning environments as well as different specialized studies packages and elective subjects for the students to choose between.
44 Bauman 2001, p. 125.
45 The Danish Ministry of Education . *The Upper Secondary School Reform 2003*.
46 Bernstein 1983, p. 147.
47 See also The Danish Ministry of Education 2009.

national goals. Therefore, we find it reasonable to claim that the Danish upper secondary teachers *still*[48] have great autonomy, especially compared to the USA. According to Berliner and Nichols[49], the way in which a lack of autonomy, high stake testing and stringent top-down control erode and distorts the integrity of the American education system. Although Denmark is not in this situation, Reform 2005 challenges the individual autonomy in favour of the "collective".

New teacher challenges in an era of reform

As mentioned before, Reform 2005 challenges the traditional teacher role. The Danish upper secondary teachers have to learn many new competencies. This is also the case in many other western and eastern countries, where teachers' roles are being expanded.[50] One of the demands in Reform 2005 – among others – is that teachers must participate in *teacher teams*. It is required that teachers from different faculties work together to design curricular activities such as the *General Study Preparation*. The teachers are also encouraged to inspire each other with new pedagogical ideas. We will follow Robin Alexander and define the term *pedagogical* as:

> "…the act of teaching together with its attendant discourse of educational theories, values, evidence and justifications. It is what one needs to know, and the skills one needs to command, in order to make and justify the many different kinds of decisions of which teaching is constituted".[51]

General Study Preparation (GSP) has been introduced with Reform 2005. GSP is a collaboration between subjects among and across the humanistic subjects, scientific subjects and social science subjects. The aim of GSP is to help students use their knowledge from different subjects in interdisciplinary projects. By using subjects from different tra-

---

48 We are aware of many of the new procedures the teachers must follow. For instance they must evaluate their doings and results and use different teaching methods etc.
49 Berliner & Nichols 2007.
50 Easthope & Easthope 2000; Bartlett 2004.
51 Alexander 2008, p.47.

ditions (humanistic sciences, natural sciences and social sciences), the purpose is to advance the students' creative abilities, critical sense and to strengthen their ability to reflect and take responsibility for their surroundings and their own development.

The establishment of teacher teams has been seen as one solution to achieve these goals. The intentions are that the teachers, working in teacher teams, *collectively* plan and prepare GSP as well as sharing and discussing pedagogical thoughts and ideas. At best these thoughts and ideas constitute a basis for general pedagogical development. This can be seen as a kind of revolution in the history of the Danish Upper Secondary School. The long tradition and culture of noninterference and equal status among the Danish upper secondary teachers is now being challenged.

Empirical studies show that many teachers find the reform rather radical, because it challenges the "freedom of method" of the individual teacher.[52] In the past teachers may have assisted one another or shared materials and methods, but the work of the teachers was primarily independent in nature. Reform 2005 seems to create an opportunity for teachers to participate in *genuine interdependent joint work*, as Little calls it.[53] We agree with Little as we consider the term *team* "has remained conceptually amorphous and ideologically sanguine",[54] and that it is based on the assumption that it will indubitably enhance the collective capacity of groups or institutions.

Moving from an individual teacher's isolation for the benefit of the collective culture automatically assumes an improvement of the teachers' pedagogical competencies. For that reason, we find it important to ask how professionalism is impacted in this particular situation and what problems teachers may face in the adjustment to the new conditions. Whether the consequences of the implementation of teacher teams in the upper secondary schools reflect a tendency towards professionalism or de-professionalism will, we would argue, to a great extent depend on how teachers cope with the new demands.[55] To begin, we will focus on the phenomenon professionalism.

---

52 Beck & Frederiksen 2007.
53 Little 1990.
54 Little 1990 p. 509.
55 Kelchtermans & Ballet 2002; Kelchtermans 2005.

Professionalism – what is at stake?

Professionalism is a commonly used term. But what does it mean to be professional? Inspired by Carr [56] five commonly cited criteria of professionalism can be articulated: (I) the professions provide a public service, (II) they involve theoretical as well as practical grounded expertise, (III) they have a distinct ethical dimension which calls for expression in a code of practice, (IV) they require regulation and organization, and (V) professional practitioners require a high degree of individual autonomy for effective practice.

Using this analytical "tool" we will particularly bring (II) and (V) into focus and discuss these issues related to our research question. It does not mean that we consider the other issues as irrelevant, not at all, but it is not our intention to discuss these in this paper. In this context, we find it particularly relevant to focus on (II) and (IV) since the reform puts the classical teacher's role under pressure. New theoretical claims are at stake (II) when the teacher's individual autonomy is challenged by the collective (V).

(II): Today, it is not enough that teachers have knowledge of their subject matter and pedagogical knowledge based on their own practical experiences. Reform 2005 demands that the upper secondary teachers increase their knowledge of pedagogy, their competencies to support learners, their ability to work with GSP and their understanding of the social and cultural dimensions of education in the knowledge society. Never before has the Danish upper secondary teacher been confronted with such comprehensive pedagogical demands.[57] The shift from the "classical" teacher, a teacher who finds identity in the subject matter(s) he/she teaches, to the "creative" teacher, who possesses a myriad of competencies and theoretical pedagogical knowledge, is one of the goals with Reform 2005. In a nutshell, the creative ethos marks, as Florida[58] says, a departure from the conformist ethos because it disrupts existing patterns of life and thoughts and challenges old habits, routines, unreflective tacit knowledge and experiences.

Based on Carr's reflections,[59] a way for teachers to increase their

---

56 Carr 2000, p.23.
57 Damberg et al. 2006
58 Florida 2004, pp. 31-33.
59 Carr 2000, Carr 2003.

professionalism is to strengthen their judgments and deliberations. It requires that the teachers develop knowledge of phronesis,[60] which is practical wisdom. Practical wisdom or phronesis is concerned with what can be otherwise, with things that change. According to Aristotle, only the person who is morally virtuous will be able to be practically wise and employ wise judgements. A wise person seeks the "truth", but truth in the service of action. We are not speaking about a metaphysical truth. On the contrary, we focus on what seems to be appropriate in the situation, and of course, it depends on the situation. Like Rorty's 'ironist' a practical wise teacher has continuing doubts about the "truth" and knows she never will find it. However, she always looks for a new and more appropriate vocabulary:[61] a new vocabulary that allows her to see things differently.

Aristotle distinguishes between different forms of knowledge: episteme, techne and phronesis. It does not mean that the teacher cannot be informed by new scientific findings (episteme).

For instance the diagnosis of Attention Deficit Hyperactivity Disorder (ADHD) has helped many teachers to understand why some students have trouble concentrating more than a few minutes at a time. If teachers learn about new and fruitful methods of teaching and vice versa (techne) it can also inform teacher's judgements on how to teach appropriately in the situation depending on goals, students' needs and the context.

(V): To be able to be "creative" according to Reform 2005, teachers must participate in teams. As mentioned before this change challenges individual autonomy. The positive aspects are that colleagues can play "the devil's advocate" and challenge the individual teacher's beliefs. To do that, it is important that teachers develop a pedagogical vocabulary.[62] If not, how would they be able to discuss pedagogical issues? A common frame is needed.

The following questions seem interesting: What if the teachers are not able to account for their actions? What if they are not able to discuss professional pedagogical matters and will not be able to develop *practical*

---

60 Aristotle 1976.
61 Rorty 1989, p. 73.
62 Schmidt 1999.

wisdom? Do the teachers "have time enough" to learn all these new aspects and are they willing to commit themselves to the work it takes to change?

What problems can arise as a result of the participation in teacher teams? What about the dominant political discourses - the discourses which pay tribute to all that seems to have an effect on our nation's ability to compete on the global market - will they have impact on the way teachers act and work in teams? When we speak about wise decisions, it is moreover interesting to reflect on what can be judged as wise today. Is it possible to analyze as an assumed positive ideal? Or is it something we only can be aware of, when our code of ethics is overstepped? We do not have the answers but ask questions that point to the complexity at stake.

De-professionalism or re-professionalism?

Learning takes time and learning can be frustrating. Every learning process has an incentive dimension, as Illeris[63] points out, and this incentive dimension has a close connection to the content and social dimensions of learning. Reform 2005, as described above, entails a lot of new challenges for the teachers and requires a great deal of learning and change in the daily routines. In other words, there are new content or procedures to learn. The social dimension of learning is also being confronted, as also mentioned above, since it is now required that teachers from different faculties must work together to create interdisciplinary lessons. But what about the incentive learning dimension?

In recent research there is widespread discourse about *teacher stress* that is often connected to the implementation of government policies.[64] This phenomenon is in the educational literature also referred to as an *intensification* of teacher work. Building on previous studies done by Larson[65] and Apple[66], Hargreaves[67] summarizes the propositions of the *intensification thesis* in the following way:

---

63 Illeris 2007.
64 Hargreaves 2005; Kelchtermans 2005; Troman 2000; Van Veen 2003, Vandenberghe & Huberman 1999.
65 Larson 1980.
66 Apple 1986.
67 Hargreaves 1992.

1. Intensification leads to reduced time for relaxation during the working day, including "no time at all" for lunch.
2. Intensification leads to lack of time to renew one's skills and keep up with one's field
3. Intensification creates chronic and persistent overload (as compared with the temporary overload that is sometimes experienced in meeting deadlines) which reduces areas of personal discretion, inhibits involvement in and control over longer-term planning, and fosters dependency on externally produced materials and expertise.
4. Intensification leads to reductions in the *quality* of service, as corners are cut to save time.
5. Intensification leads to enforced diversification of expertise and responsibility to cover personnel shortages, which can in turn create excessive dependency on outside expertise and further reductions in the quality of service.
6. Intensification creates and reinforces scarcities of preparation time.
7. Intensification is voluntarily supported by many teachers and misrecognized as professionalism.

Paradoxically, it is exactly this tendency towards an increasing intensification of teacher's work, created by an "ideology of professionalism", that can lead to de-professionalizing and de-skilling of teachers:

> "Intensification goes hand in hand with de-professionalization as a teacher's job is no longer conceived of as holistic but rather as a sequence of separated tasks and assignments. The skills that seem to be important are those that are technical and executive"[68]

A central question emerges: What about the implementation of formally organized teacher teams in the Danish upper secondary schools today? Do teacher teams contribute to the intensification of teacher's work, or are teacher teams a "buffer mechanism" making it easier for individual teachers to cope with the new reform demands? The outcome is not easy to predict. Since the implementation of teacher teams is decided by the school administration, teachers might experience it as

---

68 Ballet et al. 2006 p. 211.

an artificial form of *contrived collegiality*.[69] In other words, it is not a relief but a burden.

However, it appears more complex than that. For a deeper understanding we will be following the refinements of the intensification thesis proposed by Ballet et al.[70] and Ballet & Kelchtermans'.[71] Building on several empirical studies[72], they introduce the core concept of *experience of intensification* to understand the processes involved in the implementation of government policies in schools.

In the refinements of Apple's thesis they argue that the sources of intensification are not only external. Instead there are *multiple sources of intensification*. To a great extent it is also the single teacher that can be a source of the increased pressure.

This is also a point made by Hargreaves:

> "Intensification may not impact on all teachers in the same way. It may be felt particularly keenly by those teachers who are, because of their own commitments or work circumstances (e.g., full-time rather than part-time), rather more work-centered than their colleagues, and it may be felt less keenly by others".[73]

Secondly, they mention that the intensification impact is *mediated*. It means that the cultural and structural characteristics of the school and the interpretations of the pressures made by the teachers have a lot to say in how the impact is felt and dealt with. Kelchtermans[74] calls it a "filtering" of experiences through the teacher's *personal interpretive framework*. So "the "steering" impact of external policies on teachers is not always straightforward or linear".[75]

Finally, Ballet et al. make it clear – and this is a central point – that the intensification impact is *differentiated* and may lead to de-professionalizing and de-skilling. Instead we might see tendencies toward *re-*

---

69 Hargreaves 1991; 1992; Little 1990.
70 Ballet et al. 2006.
71 Ballet & Kelchtermans 2008.
72 See also Kelchtermans 2007.
73 Hargreaves 1992 p.104.
74 Kelchtermans 1993.
75 Ballet & Kelchtermans 2008 p. 48.

professionalization in the strategies teachers use to cope with the new demands:

> "Teachers differ in the ways in which they cope with the changes and the accompanying stress and other emotions. Changes are always interpreted and although the space for reaction is limited by the specific (school) context, teachers often cope in a creative way"[76]

In this connection they also speak of teachers' *micropolitical literacy*, that is, teachers "read" and "write" their own working conditions in particular ways.[77] This may also be the case in the Danish context. Teacher stress is certainly also a big issue in the Danish schools. Some of the uncertainties that emerge in the implementation of teacher teams, e.g. questions about how teachers should work together and how they might design interdisciplinary projects, are experienced as additional work or manipulating what they already do well. This does not lead to *creative* teaching but rather to more "conservative" teaching styles.

On the other hand, teachers may begin to develop micropolitical literacy and be able to sort out what is important and what is less important. In this sense, we can speak of a kind of re-professionalization as a consequence of Reform 2005.

Conclusion

It is still too soon to evaluate whether the implementation of teacher teams in the Danish Upper Secondary School will be a success or not. In this paper we argued for a balanced view on this phenomenon. Based on a critical perspective we have discussed what the possible future might look like. The intentions of Reform 2005 are to professionalize teachers, but the consequence may be the opposite, if the teachers have to do more in less time. This intensification of teacher work may therefore result in *de-professionalism*. However, it depends on how the schools and the teachers handle the new reform demands.

If teacher teams contribute to the *professionalism* of Danish upper sec-

---

76 Ballet et al. 2006 p. 218.
77 Kelchtermans & Ballet 2002.

ondary teachers, then Reform 2005 will challenge old ineffective routines and habits by presenting new views that may result in increased and informed *practical wisdom*. This will require Danish upper secondary teachers to develop a common pedagogical language so that they are able to articulate their experiences and share new and fruitful ideas. Today, such a vocabulary needs to be enhanced in the Danish upper secondary schools. Only the future will tell if teachers are able to acquire such a vocabulary. Teachers' willingness and their abilities to be informed by theoretical as well as practical knowledge may assist teachers from different faculties who will work together to design curricular activities such as the course, General Study Preparation.

References

Alexander, R. (2008): *Essays on Pedagogy*. London: Routledge.

Apple, M.W. (1986): *Teachers and texts: A political economy of class and gender relations in education*. New York: Routledge.

Aristotle (1976): *The Ethics of Aristotle: The Nicomachean Ethics*. London: Penguin Classics.

Ballet, K. & Kelchtermans, G. (2008): Workload and willingness to change: disentangling the experience of intensification. In: *Journal of Curriculum Studies*, 40, 1, 47-67.

Ballet, K., Kelchtermans, G. & Loughran, J. (2006): Beyond intensification towards scholarship of practice: analysing changes in teachers' work lives. In: *Teachers and Teaching – Theory and Practice*, 12, 2, 209-229.

Bartlett, L. (2004): Expanding teacher work roles: a resource for retention or a recipe for overwork? In: *Journal of Education Policy*, 19, 5, 565-582.

Bauman, Z. (2001): *The Individualized Society*. Cambridge: Polity Press.

Beck, S. & Hansen, D. R. (2009): Teacher generations in an era of reform. In: *US-China Education Review*, 6, 8, 1-16.

Beck, S. Frederiksen, L. (2007): From loose to tight couplings. In: *International Journal of Management in Education*, 2, 1, 220-239.

Beck, U. & Beck-Gernsheim, E. (2001): *Individualization*. London: Sage.

Berliner, D.C. & Nichols, S.L. (2007): *How High Stakes Testing Corrupts America's Schools*. Cambridge: Harvard Education Press.

Bernstein, R. J. (1983): *Beyond Objectivism and Relativism: Science, Hermeneutics, and Praxis*. Philadelphia: University of Pennsylvania Press.

Carr, D. (2000): *Professionalism and Ethics in Teaching*. London: Routledge Falmer.

Carr, D. (2003): *Making Sense of Education. An introduction to the philosophy and theory of education and teaching.* London: RoutledgeFalmer.

Cochran-Smith (2004): Taking Stock in 2004: Teacher Education in Dangerous Times. In: *Journal of Teacher Education,* 55, 3, 3-7.

Damberg, E., Dolin, J. & Ingerslev, G.H.: Eds. (2006): *Gymnasiepædagogik - En grundbog.* København: Hans Reitzels Forlag.

Danish Ministry of Education (2003): *The Upper Secondary School Reform 2003.* http://www.uvm.dk.

Danish Ministry of Education (2009): *Upper Secondary Education.* http://www.uvm.dk.

Day, C. (1999): *Developing Teachers: The challenge of Lifelong Learning.* London: Routledge.

Easthope, C. & G. Easthope (2000): Intensification, Extension and Complexity of Teachers' Workload. In: *British Journal of Sociology of Education,* 21, 1, 43-58.

European Commission (2009): Directorate-General for Education and Culture. http://www.see-educoop.net/education_in/pdf/01-en_principles_en.pdf (March 10, 2009)

Hargreaves, A. (1991): Contrived collegiality: the micropolitics of teacher collaboration. In: Blase, J. (ed.): *The Politics of Life in Schools: Power, Conflict, and Cooperation.* Thousand Oaks, California: Corwin Press.

Hargreaves, A. (1992): Time and teachers' work: an analysis of the intensification thesis. In: *Teachers College Record,* 94, 1, 87-108.

Hargreaves, A. (2005): Educational change takes ages: Life, career and generational factors in teachers' emotional responses to educational change. In: *Teaching and Teacher Education,* 21, 8, 967-983.

Illeris, K. (2007): *How we learn: learning and non-learning in school and beyond.* London: Routledge.

Kelchtermans, G. (2005): Teachers' emotions in educational reforms: Self-understanding, vulnerable commitment and micropolitical literacy. In: *Teaching and Teacher Education,* 21, 995-1006.

Kelchtermans, G. & Ballet, K. (2002): Micropolitical literacy: reconstructing a neglected dimension in teacher development. In: *International Journal of Educational Research,* 37, 755-767.

Lading, Åse (2006) *Vi er jo kolleger, ikke konkurrenter... - en analyse af moderniserede gymnasielæreres strategier i grupper.* Ph.d.-afhandling. Institut for Filosofi, Pædagogik og Religionsstudier. Syddansk Universitet, Odense.

Larson, M.S. (1980): Proletarianization and Educated Labor. In: *Theory and*

Society, 9, 1, 131-175.

Little, J.W. (1990): The Persistence of Privacy: Autonomy and Initiative in Teachers' Professional Relations. In: *Teachers College Record*, 91, 4, 509-536.

Prosser, M. & Trigwell, K. (2001): *Understanding Learning and Teaching. The Experience in Higher Education.* Buckingham: Open University Press.

Rorty, R. (1989): *Contingency, irony, and solidarity.* Cambridge: Cambridge University Press.

Schmidt, L.H. (1999): *Diagnosis III. Pædagogiske forhold.* København: Danmarks Pædagogiske Institut.

Troman, G. (2000): Teacher stress in the low-trust society. In: *British Journal of Sociology of Education*, 21, 3, 331-353.

Tørnæs, U. (2004) Åbning af udstilling om gymnasieskolen. I: Damberg, E. (ed.): *En uddannelsesreform fylder 100 år.* Gymnasiepædagogik, nr. 49. Odense: Dansk Institut for Gymnasiepædagogik, Syddansk Universitet.

Vandenberghe, R. & Huberman, A.M. (eds.) (1999): *Understanding and Preventing Teacher Burnout: A Sourcebook of International Research and Practice.* Cambridge: Cambridge University Press.

Van Veen, K. (2003): *Teachers' emotions in a context of reforms.* Ph.D. thesis, Nijmegen University, The Netherlands.

Lifelong, Life-wide and Life-deep Learning: Utilizing the Lens of HIV and AIDS[78] in South Africa

Shirley Walters

Introduction

Adult and lifelong learning in sub-Saharan Africa cannot ignore HIV and AIDS. In sub-Saharan Africa none of us is unaffected by HIV and AIDS. It weaves through our personal, political and pedagogical lives. HIV and AIDS highlight some of the most difficult social, economic, cultural and personal issues that any adult educators have to confront, therefore, increasingly people are recognizing the importance of understanding both academic and non-academic literature to grapple with pedagogies of HIV and AIDS.

According to Steinberg (2008), a journalist, political scientist and author, about 2.1 million people died of AIDS in sub-Saharan Africa in 2006 while another 25 million are living with HIV. In South Africa, about 13% of the population is HIV positive, with an adult prevalence rate of 18.8%. Some 800 - 1000 die of AIDS on an average day. And the epidemic is spreading at about 1500 new infections a day. (Lees 2008:1) In his excellent, textured, three year study in a South African rural village, Lusikisiki, Steinberg pursued the question, why are people dying en masse when they are within a short distance of treatment? Through his book, the complex inter-play between politics, culture, economics, gender relations, power, and history, are described as he draws out the intricate realities of the place and people of Lusikisiki. However, his

---

78 This paper draws on work I am developing with Heather Ferris, who works both in Canada and Southern Africa in relation to HIV and AIDS, and other trauma. She has written a book "Someone I love died" for use by young people. I appreciate feedback on drafts of this paper from Linzi Manicom and Heather Ferris.

analysis does not stay with the specificities of one rural village as he skillfully shines light on similar social dynamics that exist within all societies in Africa and elsewhere. The complexities of human behaviour that he describes graphically illustrate the challenges for adult and lifelong learning.

Lees (2008) in his very useful doctoral study on 'rethinking AIDS education' echoes Freire (1993:25) who states that "Humanization has always been humankind's central problem". Lees' study contends that 're-thinking our understanding of the AIDS pandemic allows us to see that AIDS is about people, not simply about the virus' and he uses critical and post-colonial frames of analysis to question the interventions to date and asks about 'who we would like to become as individuals, communities, a nation, and a species' (Lees:2). He questions how well we understand the lives and behaviors of people - hence the value of turning to a range of literature and other sources to elucidate our understandings. One such book is by Sindiwe Magona (2008) who illustrates the intricacies of gender relations amongst a group of 4 middle class, Cape Town based, black women and their partners, whose close friend, Beauty, has died of AIDS, contracted from her 'unfaithful husband'. The story highlights the deeply gendered nature of HIV and AIDS as each of the main characters struggles to assert their friend, Beauty's gift to them, which is to take control of their sexual relationships with their partners in order 'to live a long life'. The questions for this paper then are: What can be gleaned from the challenges of HIV and AIDS? How does this scourge force us to think differently about the theories and practices of adult education and lifelong learning?

I reflect back on approaches that Heather Ferris and I have developed over several years. From these experiences, our observations are that working with people infected and affected by HIV and AIDS brings into sharp focus the need for pedagogical approaches to:

1. Include male and female, children and adults across generations, for all ages (i.e. lifelong learning);
2. Recognize the importance of sustainable livelihoods and systemic issues in a life-wide approach (i.e. life wide learning); and
3. Work with deeply personal issues relating to death and sexual relations which tap into the cultural, spiritual, and intimate aspects of people's lives (i.e. life deep learning).

Examples from adult learning in South Africa

South Africa's position as a land of struggle and hope is fairly well known. Many aspects of its economic, political and social life are strongly framed by the dualities of struggle and hope. In 1994, the country took centre stage internationally when Nelson Mandela became the first president of a democratic state, after decades of sustained popular struggle against divisive and destructive apartheid rule. The country entered the global economy as a democratic, free and hopeful country. The relatively "peaceful" nature of the transition gave South Africa beacon status on the continent, lighting up vistas from struggle to hope.

A key observation for adult learning within a lifelong learning framework, in a middle income country like South Africa, is that a very large proportion of the population comprises young people. South Africa's population of 48 million is predominantly young and black with 51% below the age of 25. The demographic profile is diametrically opposite to that of most of the developed economies. In addition, the average life expectancy of the population is falling, compared to its rise in the North. These fundamental demographic differences between countries of the South and of the North are very significant and challenge us from a global perspective to broaden our understandings of adult and lifelong learning. Grappling with these differences, is made all the more difficult because of the hegemony of 'Northern' or Eurocentric adult education scholarship.

In South Africa, the majority black population is suffering from the inequitable distribution of wealth that is apartheid's legacy; is more likely to be unemployed; and receives less schooling, of a poorer standard, than their white counterparts. Despite that, members of this majority are more and better educated at school than their fathers and mothers. The potential and actual adult learners speak many languages (there are 11 official languages); for the majority of them, English, the main language of adult learning, is not their first language. They live in areas that differ widely from one another, some with very high rates of HIV and TB and low life expectancy, robbing South African society of large numbers of skilled people it badly needs; others are relatively safe from killer diseases and have a life expectancy comparable to that of developed economies. There is a rapidly growing black middle class.

The needs for adult learning programmes inevitably cross a vast economic and social spectrum, from the most basic to the most advanced.

The examples that I will draw on come from experiences of the majority of the population. But in highlighting the lives of poor women and men, whose lives have been ravaged by the dual effects of globalization and HIV and AIDS, this paper does not intend to reproduce the images of suffering, passivity, ignorance, and stigma which often dominate the representations of African people in the media. Similar to Ida Susser's (2009) approach in her recent work, I hope that the ingenuity and agency of local people is not lost, while not underestimating the forces of economic globalization that shape all of our lives.

I will start by giving short composite profiles of typical learners within the general adult basic education system (ABET). I will then provide two examples of HIV and AIDS focused training programmes. My purpose is to show how approaches to combat HIV and AIDS, have relevance for the system more broadly:[79]

1. *Sindi* is a married woman with three children. She has earned a living making mud building blocks for her neighbours, selling second hand clothes and doing domestic work. Her husband gets temporary jobs in people's homes. He has a drinking problem. Therefore Sindi is the primary earner and care-giver. She left school in Grade 7 because her friends were all leaving to try to find work. Her motivation to attend ABET classes was to get a better job. She now is employed as a nurse assistant. She plans to study hard to save enough money so that her children can get tertiary education.

2. *Rachel* spoke of her supportive mother who helped her during her early years in school. Her father died when she was very young. After she had moved to live with relatives, her schooling was affected because of the work that she had to do in their home and because she was sexually abused. She dropped out of school after this incident. When she was older she had her own family and was building a good home for them,

---

[79] Composite profiles drawn from Vaughn John "*Communities of learning and action?: a case study of the Human Rights, Democracy and Development Project, 1999-2005*, Doctoral Thesis 2009, University of Kwa-Zulu Natal; June Roodt 2007 *An exploration of learning by women in the clothing and textile industry within the context of the national skills development strategy*. A thesis in partial fulfillment of the Masters in Education, University of Western Cape, South Africa

which was destroyed through political violence. She is now single and is a member of the development structure and peace committee in her area.

3. *Zelpha* left school in Grade 2 because her father said that he did not have money to educate her 'for someone else' (i.e. a future husband). After her parents died she looked after her siblings but could not support their education from her meagre income as a farm worker. She married but divorced her husband because of physical abuse. She is active in her church. Her three sisters have died in recent years and left all their children in her care. She is proud that she is a spiritual person and has skills in sewing and gardening which she shares with others.

4. *Zuzile's* father passed away when he was young. He says that rather than going to school he had to take care of his uncle's livestock. He went to the city where he worked as a cook and assistant to a bricklayer. He has also run his own business selling chips and fruit. Although he had no schooling he married someone with Grade 12 whom he met in church. He eventually returned to his home community where he joined ABET classes – his ABET level 2 certificate helped get him a job in a hospital kitchen. As the only man who was attending ABET classes he was accused of being interested in other people's wives.

5. *Elizabeth* works in a clothing factory. Her mother worked as a cleaner also in a clothing factory and worked overtime every night. Her father was a mechanic. She spoke of her mother struggling financially as her father had extra-marital relationships and did not support the family adequately. Her mother was physically abused by her father. Elizabeth is now divorced with 2 sons. Her abusive husband refuses to move out of their house. Her eldest child has finished school and is currently working at the same company. The youngest is at school and abuses drugs. She has participated in various training programmes at work.

For all of the learners, attempting to create sustainable livelihoods is central to their participation in learning. The majority are women who are often the key 'bread winners'; have to manage oppressive, abusive gender relations; are active in religious, community or political structures; are having to absorb additional burdens through fostering children of deceased family members; are aspiring for better conditions for their children while dealing with the traumas that punctuate their lives; and also show enormous resilience.

These learners are the same ones who are extraordinarily susceptible to HIV and AIDS. As Susser (2009: 45) says, "….biology, culture, social organization, low incomes and lack of services conspire to render women extraordinarily susceptible to HIV infection". I turn now to descriptions of two training courses which were explicitly designed for caregivers and volunteers affected and infected with HIV and AIDS. They illustrate the need for approaches which are lifelong, life wide and life deep. The first example also argues for the importance of the 'life long and life deep' learning of the facilitators or educators themselves.

Example 1: HIV and AIDS Workshops for Caregivers and Volunteers[80]

Heather Ferris, the facilitator of a series of HIV and AIDS workshops for training of community-based caregivers in rural and urban areas of Southern Africa says:

> At the first 4 day long workshop we were told that the rate of infection is very high and people are in denial. Every story involves a number of family members who have died. It becomes the norm and I no longer feel surprised. It is more the question of how many than shock at a family death. The theme for the first day was personal loss so that the participants could understand their own losses. They were reminded to breathe deeply and during sharing, to listen without responding. They started with a personal loss line and then gathered in groups of five to hear stories. N and I circulated reminding people to breathe or to gently place a hand on their shoulders. After sharing their stories we focused on where in their bodies they felt the loss. There were tears as they breathed fully into their pain and then a sense of relief for most people. They were introduced to Capacitar[81] holds (healing techniques for trauma release), which they practiced in pairs recognizing which hold had the most benefit. The connections between people became palpable.

---

80 These are taken from notes from the facilitator, Heather Ferris.
81 This refers to methodologies developed by Capacitar and its co-director, Dr Pat Cane. See for example, "Trauma, healing and Transformation', Capacitar 2000, and other hand books.

Some comments from workshop participants:

> A 40 year old man described the constraining gender norms of grieving and the benefits of embodied learning when he said: "I agree that culturally men are taught not to cry when they suffer from grief. When I lost my wife, I first cried. Immediately after that I thought that as a man I am not supposed to cry, because I have to keep myself strong irrespective of how painful my heart is. After the funeral I thought about all the good things my wife used to do in taking care of my children and myself and how much love she had for the whole extended family. After that I started to think that there is no-one who will ever replace her in my heart. I felt so heartbroken and immediately felt pains in my whole body. I could not handle the situation I broke into tears and cried bitterly. After that I felt so much relief in my body, not that the pain of loss was gone, but relief of pain in my body. This training has taught me to listen to my body."

> A 28 year old woman expressed the importance of learning across generations when she said: "To lose my mom and dad was such a terrible nightmare. I am the oldest child who has to look after three children. I can see that the workshop is helping me deal with my grief first and also helping me handle the orphans that I am looking after." A Grandmother said: "I am a grandmother of 8 orphans as I lost my two daughters a year ago due to AIDS. It is quite hard for me to cope with the 8 children in terms of comforting them." The workshop helped people to recognize their own trauma first and then to help the children work through theirs.

All generations and genders are infected and affected by HIV and AIDS. The senses of death, loss, trauma, are deeply personal and the facilitators have to confront their own loss and pain as part of learning to help others. The healing processes for the educators are critical to them being able to do the work. This resonates with the realization by Freire and many others, that as adult educators we cannot leave ourselves 'at the door'. We have to be fully present with our own humanity. Working with our own and others' trauma demands 'life deep learning' for both ourselves as the educators and for the learners; working across all generations is necessary from young children, through to grandmothers and grandfathers.

Example 2: Women's Leadership Development course in Masiphumele[82]
A second example of a local programme for the development of women's leadership for working with HIV and AIDS related trauma, demonstrates the importance of a holistic, life-wide, approach to the curriculum.

This was a one month full time course for 17 unemployed women, who were working in their impoverished community as volunteers. They wanted to help others who were also living in poverty and confronting trauma through the loss of friends and family to AIDS. The facilitator developed the curriculum through a process of immersion with the community over a six-month period - several days a week, listening, engaging, and supporting women and their organizations. It was soon clear that HIV and AIDS is integral to life, and cannot be separated from achieving forms of sustainable livelihoods. The curriculum covered team and personal development, through a range of participatory approaches, including the setting up of small businesses. Skills building sessions were woven through the course and covered: HIV and AIDS; gender relations; communication skills; English conversation; personal development; financial management; entrepreneurial skills; time management; goal setting; problem solving; team building; healthy life style including bicycle riding skills; and management of meetings.

The group worked together to analyze the needs in the community relating to HIV and AIDS and developed a proposal to provide care to those who were infected. Ultimately this was taken up by one group while another developed a child-care facility to care for the children of people who were not well, which five years later houses over 100 children each day.

The course aspired to hold a number of intrinsic values, which are well known to adult educators. They included feminist popular education principles of 'seeing with the heart and speaking from the heart'; valuing mind, body and spirit equally in the activities; and encouraging silence, contemplation and reflection as a necessary part of each session. After an intense month together, an external facilitator interacted with the group to hear what it was that they had found most useful - the women made collages to convey their feelings. These were kept by the

---

82 These are taken from notes of the facilitator, Heather Ferris.

women and used to decorate the venue when they graduated to show people what they had learned. These included their growing confidence and understanding of gender equality; leadership; helping others and being willing to try different approaches. They spoke of being active and 'going for it'. They were unanimous about the value of financial management. They had never before kept account of their money.

The graduation celebration involved all women speaking in front of the crowd. They were very encouraging of one another mostly through songs and dancing. A most telling statement was made by one of the women, which reinforces Jim Lees' observation of people's sense of dehumanization, "Some people think we are animals. We aren't, you know, we are human beings; in this course we were treated like human beings".

This workshop illustrates holistic approaches to adult learning which are 'life-wide' and 'life deep' which acknowledge the economic and systemic necessities; the personal skills required; the need participants have to belong and experience their humanness; and the need to build solidarity both with one another and also within the broader community. The course recognized the help the women needed to understand how to access state resources, like social welfare grants, use of health clinic services, and so on. The individual was connected to society like a spider in its web.

Discussion

Thinking about the profiles of the average adult learners and examples of HIV and AIDS training workshops, what are some useful ways of thinking about adult and lifelong learning? While these examples come from South Africa, it is important to acknowledge that in the majority world many of issues may vary in some ways but are essentially the same. I will make six concluding points:

1. Knud Illeris (2007) emphasizes that central to learning is the interaction between the motivation (or incentive) of a learner and the content (curriculum). Key questions for educators are: who is the learner, why are they there, what are their life circumstances? Successful learning occurs when these questions are taken into account. Therefore, successful learning systems or programmes cannot 'leave the identities of the learners at the door'. Canadian scholar, Jenny Horsman (1999), highlights

the centrality of violence and its impact on learning[83] and how essential it is to acknowledge this in the ways we design and facilitate learning. In a context like that in South Africa, where violence is endemic for the majority of the population, educators and learners need to understand how to work with trauma (their own or others'), if they are to overcome the enormous barriers to successful learning which violence of all kinds can cause. The necessary 'healing processes' need to be incorporated to enable learners and facilitators to be 'fully human'. This highlights the critical importance of educators who are well trained and supported.

2. Patriarchy is alive and well with gender violence and abuse being endemic, which emphasizes the importance of understanding oppressive gender relations in their complexity and being encouraged to resist and overcome them, working together with men and women, girls and boys. Feminist popular education principles and methodologies of 'seeing with the heart and speaking from the heart'; valuing mind, body and spirit equally in the approaches and methods; and encouraging silence, contemplation and reflection as a necessary part of learning from where individuals and collectives can draw new strength for the struggles ahead, are essential; as are the participatory methods for assisting people understand critically how their local material conditions are shaped by the transnational and global forces – they need to understand that they are like spiders within complex webs.

Feminist popular education (Manicom and Walters 1997; Walters and Manicom 1996; Fernandes 2003) has developed around the world to support poor, marginalized women to challenge their subordinate positions and conditions, individually and collectively. In the current global conjuncture, where fundamentalisms, economic hardships (exacerbated by the financial meltdown) and authoritarianisms of various kinds are widespread, the need for adult educators to place the subordinate position of women at the centre of their pedagogy echoes in the African context. Feminist popular educators, in the last ten to fifteen years, have been developing deeper understandings of methodologies to work with the 'head, the heart and the hands' to help learners both understand their situations and to take actions to change them. There

---

83 Her very useful website is www.learningandviolence.net

appears to be growing convergence in the literature on transformative learning and feminist popular education. (See for example Merriam and Ntseane 2008)

3. While there has been a rapid increase in the relative size of the black middle class in places like South Africa, and there is a black President in the USA, the economy and the multi-lateral global organizations are dominated by white people with urban, Eurocentric views. In this context, post-colonial theory (see for example, Said 1978, Mohanty 2003; Spivak 1990; Tikly 1999; Chilisa 2005), which is much more than anti-racism, is a useful lens with which to analyse adult and lifelong learning. It focuses attention on much deeper and longer histories of colonisation which have left deep footprints across the length and breadth of the African continent, and many other parts of the world.

As Julia Preece (2009) says, for countries of the South to challenge dominant perceptions, we need explanatory theoretical frameworks that make sense of our particular historical contexts. This includes re-narrating the experiences of colonisation from the viewpoints of the colonised, and the implications this has for adult and lifelong learning. It means recognising the impact that colonization has had on people's identities, cultures, their claims to indigenous knowledge, their experiences of racism and sexism and their ongoing effects. This includes understanding the institutional structures, textual representations and power relations that enabled domination to operate so effectively under a banner of benevolence, manifested through discourses of 'development'.

While not getting stuck, as Odora Hoppers (2009) says, "mesmerized by the cobra of colonialism", AIDS in Africa needs to be located in the historical context of colonialism that continues in new and old forms. But cultural practices, which are generative of positive self-identities, are necessary. As Lees elaborates, 'The real challenge to AIDS education in the continent is to initiate conversations that do not pathologise African people. The second challenge is to understand that the AIDS pandemic and HIV prevention are about healing more than our bodies'. As our examples help to show, there is a need for the full humanity of all people to be recognised, including the acknowledgement of the potential value of subjugated knowledges which can help to illuminate the paths ahead for alternative, sustainable ways of being and living.

4. With the shifting demographics and the changes in the roles and responsibilities of both the young and old, women and men, through many parents dying from AIDS, cross generational understanding and collaboration is essential to provide support for communities which are under severe strain. HIV and AIDS highlights the need for pedagogical approaches that can be used with learners of all ages, genders, across generations. For example, very young children can be sexually abused in line with mythologies around the curative effects of having sexual intercourse with virgins; there are growing numbers of child-headed households; and grandparents are left to support new generations of children with their own children dying of AIDS. The ability to openly discuss and debate sexual practices across social classes, cultures, religions, genders and ages, is a matter of life and death. The importance of locating adult learning within lifelong learning through philosophical and pedagogical approaches is graphically illustrated through the HIV and AIDS pandemic.

5. The world is dominated by neo-liberal economics, which have led to forms of 'casino capitalism' and 'neo-colonialism', which need to be understood in order that people are able to begin to imagine other alternatives for sustainable living in a just and caring world. The majority of people is poor, therefore analytical frameworks that are in the interests of supporting them individually and collectively, are essential. The importance of holistic approaches which integrate the centrality of sustainable livelihoods, taking into account the shifting realities and full humanity of the majority world, lead to an emphasis on learning which is lifelong, life-wide, and life-deep. Grappling with the complexities of pedagogies of HIV and AIDS can assist the processes of re-theorising adult and lifelong learning. These new understandings in turn need to inform policies and practices in the interests of the poor majority whose learning and healing is at the centre.

6. A core premise is that good teaching comes from the identity and integrity of the educator, who is concerned with the lives of the people involved, and is also concerned with our own life-long, life-wide and life-deep learning in the interests of a more just and caring planet. It is critical for us as adult educators to engage in self-reflection in order to be with students in the fabric of life. The art and heart of the educator are

one, where the connections made by good teachers are held not in their methods, but in their hearts.

If all this feels rather daunting, it may be helpful to take solace from a quote from an ancient source of Jewish religious law, The Talmud, *"Do not be daunted by the enormity of the world's grief. Do justly now. Love mercy now. Walk humbly now. You are not obliged to complete the work, but neither are you free to abandon it."*

References

Cane, Pat (2005) *Living in Wellness - Trauma Healing.* USA, Capacitar International

Chilisa, B. (2005) 'Educational research within postcolonial Africa: a critique of HIV and AIDS research in Botswana', *International Journal of Qualitative Studies in Education* Vol. 18 No. 6 November-December pp. 659 – 684

Fernandes, L. (2003) *Transforming feminist practice: Non-violence, social justice and the possibilities of a spiritualized feminism,* San Francisco, Aunt Lute Books

Freire, P. (1993) *Pedagogy of the oppressed,* London, Penguin Books

Horsman, J. (1999) *Too scared to learn: Women, violence and education,* Canada, Mc Gilligan Books

Illeris, K. (2007) *How we learn,* London and New York, Routledge

John, V. (2009) *Communities of learning and action? A case study of the Human Rights, Democracy and Development Project 1999-2005.* Unpublished. Doctor of Philosophy Thesis, University of Kwa-Zulu Natal, South Africa

Lees, J.C. (2008) *Re-thinking AIDS education: laying a new foundation for more appropriate practice in South Africa.* Unpublished Doctoral Thesis, University of Western Cape, South Africa

Magona, S. (2008) *Beauty's Gift,* Cape Town, Kwela Books

Manicom, L. and Walters, S. (1997) Feminist popular education in the light of globalization. In Walters S. (ed.) 1997 *Globalization, adult education and training: impacts and issues,* London, Zed Books

Merriam, S. and Ntseane, G. (2008) Transformational learning in Botswana: How culture shapes the process. In *Adult Education Quarterly* Vol. 58 No. 3 pp. 183 - 197

Mohanty, C. (2003) 'Under western eyes' revisited: Feminist solidarity through anticapitalist struggles. In Mohanty C. *Feminism without borders: Decolonising theory, practicing solidarity,* Durham and London, Duke University Press

Odora Hoppers, C. "The 6th Vice Chancellor's Julius Nyerere Lecture on Lifelong Learning", 3 September 2009, University of Western Cape, South Africa

Preece, J. (2009) *Lifelong learning and development. A Southern Perspective*, London, Continuum Publishing Group

Roodt, J. (2007) *An exploration of learning by women in the clothing and textile industry within the context of the national skills development strategy*. A thesis in partial fulfillment of the Masters in Education, University of Western Cape, South Africa

Said, E. (1978) *Orientalism*, New York, Vintage Books

Spivak, G.C. (ed.) (1990) *The post-colonial critic: interviews, strategies, dialogues*, New York, Routledge

Steinberg, J. (2008) *The 3 letter plague*, Cape Town and Johannesburg, Jonathan Ball Publishers

Susser, I. (2009) Aids, *sex and culture: Global politics and survival in Southern Africa*, USA / UK, Wiley-Blackwell

Tikly, L. (1999) Postcolonialism and comparative education, *International Review of Education*, 45 (5/6) pp. 603 – 621

Walters, S. and Manicom, L. (1996) *Gender in popular education: methods for empowerment*. London, Zed Books

Authors

Thomas R.S. Albrechtsen, MA in General Education, Ph.D.-student at the Institute of Philosophy, Education and the Study of Religions, University of Southern Denmark. Research fields: Sociology of education, systems theory, teachers' work, collegiality, professional development.
trsa@ifpr.sdu.dk

Christina Chaib is Associate Professor of Education at the University of Jönköping, Sweden. She is a research fellow at the Swedish National Centre for Lifelong Learning Encell (www.encell.se). Her ongoing research is about workplace related learning, focusing on the relationship between theory and practice in Advanced Vocational Education and Training (AVET), as well as mentoring at workplaces. Another field of her research interest is related to the aesthetical aspects of learning processes. Christina Chaib is presently engaged, together with 24 researchers from European countries, in a Leonardo da Vinci project dealing with validation of non-formal and informal learning.
christina.chaib@hlk.hj.se

Birthe Lund is Associate Professor and PhD at the Department of Education, Learning and Philosophy at Aalborg University. Her main research interest is innovative learning and didactics in education and business which reflect her focus on the use of a variety of media and methods within the field. She has participated in the development of a number of new master programmes and research programs within the field of innovation and innovation strategies within the public sector. She gives Master- and Ph.D-courses on innovative pedagogy and didactics and design of innovation and creativity in education and business. Ass.Prof. Lund is member of the research group FIU (Forskning i undervisning og uddannelseskulturer) (Research in Education and Cultures of learning).
bl@learning.oau.dk

Dipl. Päd. Monika E. Fischer is a research staff member of the Department of Adult Education at the Goethe University of Frankfurt. Research interests include adult's biographies of learning as well as modernization and adult education. She is currently working on a doctoral thesis on the relevance of "space" as a concept and object within educational research and practice.
Monika.Fischer@em.uni-frankfurt.de

Petros Gougoulakis, is an Assistant Professor of education at the Department of Education, Stockholm University. He has extensive teaching experience in teacher education and Open University courses in adult learning since 1993. His PhD thesis deals with the Swedish Popular Adult Education and its most prevailing study method, the study circle. He has been involved in several research projects concerning non-formal and formal adult education in Sweden Currently, he participates in the multilateral Leonardo Da Vinci project "QF2TEACH - Qualified to Teach", which aims to determine the core competencies needed by teachers in Adult and Continuing Education in different European countries. He is one of the editors of *Vuxenantologin* [Anthology of Adult Learning], 2006.
Petros.Gougoulakis@ped.su.se

Dion Rüsselbæk Hansen, MA(Ed) in General Education, Ph.D.-student at the Institute of Philosophy, Education and Study of Religions, University of Southern Denmark; Research fields: Philosophy of education, social-analytical diagnoses of our age, discourse analysis of educational reforms and strategies of modernization, teacher education and teacher roles.
dion@ifpr.sdu.dk

Prof. Dr. Christiane Hof is Professor of Adult & Continuing Education. Department of Adult & Continuing Education.University of Frankfurt/Main.
  Research interests: Theory and practice of lifelong learning, professionalization, forms of learning and teaching.
hof@em.uni.frankfurt.de

Marianne Horsdal is Professor of educational research at the University of Southern Denmark Institute of Philosophy, Education and the Study

of Religions. Research interests include lifelong learning, life story narratives, biographical learning, democracy, identity and intercultural competences.
horsdal@ifpr.sdu.dk

Annie Aarup Jensen is Associate Professor and PhD at the Department of Education, Learning and Philosophy at Aalborg University. Her research interests include adults' learning and pedagogy in Higher Education as well as intercultural learning. She is a member of the research group FiU (Forskning i undervisning og uddannelseskulturer - Research in Education and Cultures of Learning). Ms. Aarup Jensen has participated in the development and implementation of a number of new master programmes.
aaj@learning.aau.dk

Anne Larson is Associate Professor in sociology of education at the Danish School of Education, Aarhus University (DK). She is MA in political science and PhD in sociology of education. Her main research interests are education policy and lifelong learning, including implementation of lifelong learning, and participation/non-participation in adult education from a national as well as an international comparative perspective. Anne Larson is co-convenor of the ESREA Network "Policy Studies and Politics of Education".
anne@dpu.dk

Marcella Milana is Associate Professor of adult education at the Danish School of Education University of Aarhus (DK). Her research interests include adult education policy, adult education for democratic citizenship, participation in adult education and professionalisation in the field of adult education, from national as well as international perspectives. She teaches and supervises MA students in lifelong learning. Furthermore, she is on the boards of the Nordic Comparative and International Education Society (NOCIES) and the International Society for Comparative Adult Education (ISCAE).
mami@dpu.dk

Jyri Manninen is Professor (Adult & Continuing Education) at University of Eastern Finland (www.uef.fi), Faculty of Philosophy, Department

of Education and Psychology. His main research interests are learning environments, participation in adult education, wider benefits of learning, developmental evaluation and lifelong learning policies.
jyri.manninen@uef.fi

Ingela Bergmo Prvulovic is a Ph D student of Pedagogy, at the School of Education and Communication, Jönköping University, Sweden, and furthermore connected to the National Center for Lifelong Learning (www.encell.se). Her ongoing research focuses on adult career development, counselling processes and individuals' self-managing of careers, within the context in which individuals experience and construct their own career, in times of transition and change. Ingela Bergmo Prvulovic' is presently engaged, in a Leonardo da Vinci project dealing with validation of non-formal and informal learning.
ingela.bergmo-prvulovic@hlk.hj.se

Ulla Thøgersen, Ph.D., is Assistant Professor at the Department of Education, Learning and Philosophy at Aalborg University in the northern part of Denmark. Her educational background is in philosophy, communication and learning theory. Main research areas include learning processes in organizational and educational settings viewed from philosophical perspectives on desire, passions, embodiment and speech.
ulla@learning.aau.dk

Shirley Walters is Professor at the University of Western Cape, South Africa, where she has been professor of adult and continuing education for 25 years. She is director of Division for Lifelong Learning at UWC and the chairperson of the South African Qualifications Authority. She is a scholar-activist who has been working for social justice, in South Africa and more broadly, for many years.
ferris@iafrica.com

Søren Willert is Associate Professor at the Department of Education, Learning, and Philosophy, Aalborg University. During the last four years he has been engaged in planning and implementing a pedagogically ambitious Master Programme in Organizational Coaching. During the period 1968-2006 he was attached to Dept. of Psychology, University of

Aarhus. His research interests are centered on the epistemology of professional practice and psychology of consciousness.
swi@hum.aau.dk